LESS
is
more

Facing the Impossible With Just a Little Faith

Alfredo Ballesta

WESTBOW
PRESS®
A DIVISION OF THOMAS NELSON
& ZONDERVAN

WestBow Press books may be ordered through booksellers or by contacting:

WestBow Press
A Division of Thomas Nelson & Zondervan
1663 Liberty Drive
Bloomington, IN 47403
www.westbowpress.com
844-714-3454

All Scripture quotations are taken from The Holy Bible, English Standard Version® (ESV®), Copyright © 2001 by Crossway, a publishing ministry of Good News Publishers. All rights reserved.

ISBN: 978-1-6642-1670-9 (sc)
ISBN: 978-1-6642-1671-6 (hc)
ISBN: 978-1-6642-1669-3 (e)

Library of Congress Control Number: 2020925015

Print information available on the last page.

WestBow Press rev. date: 12/16/2020

I want to thank, first and foremost, God, who has led me to experience from Him what I can now share. I also thank my wife (who helped me with the design of the cover) and she has had the patience to accompany me in every situation we have faced. Thank you, too, to each person with whom we have shared some moment of this journey of faith, trusting in Jesus, sometimes with just a little faith. Thank you!

Have you ever been in front of the ocean? Most of us enjoy nature—the sun, the water, the sand—but have you ever stopped to think about how big the ocean is compared to you? Yes, it is very big. And we are very small.

> Who has measured the waters in the hollow of his hand and marked off the heavens with a span, enclosed the dust of the earth in a measure and weighed the mountains in scales and the hills in a balance? Who has measured the Spirit of the Lord, or what man shows him his counsel? Whom did he consult, and who made him understand? Who taught him the path of justice, and taught him knowledge, and showed him the way of understanding? Behold, the nations are like a drop from a bucket, and are accounted as the dust on the scales; behold, he takes up the coastlands like fine dust. (Isaiah 40:12–15)

God is much bigger than the sea, the earth, or the sky. His greatness does not fit in our imagination. If nations are like dust to Him, how much smaller in comparison will each of us be? But nevertheless

> When I look at your heavens, the work of your fingers, the moon and the stars, which you have set in place, what is man that you are mindful of him, and the son of man that you care for him? (Psalms 8:3–4)

We can imagine that when David wrote Psalm 8 he had been observing not the sea but the sky. It was so huge! And all of that had been created by God: "the work of your fingers."

But then David realized that he himself was talking to God, that God was relating to him. And he sprouted from his lips the question that any of us can ask: "What is man that you are mindful of him, and the son of man that you care for him?"

In other words, who am I to have this high privilege of speaking to You?

Before God we are insignificant, and despite that, God has wanted to relate to us. Not only relate, but invite us to be part of what He does.

If you have already believed in Jesus, you have been reconciled to God and established a relationship with Him. It is my prayer and hope that what you are beginning to read will help you cultivate an even deeper and more fruitful relationship with our Savior.

But keep this in mind: His math is different than ours.

For Him, less is more.

You and I are fragile and insufficient. We have a poor understanding on things. Despite this, God wants to allow us to know Him and leads us to participate in His work. That implies that we may see coming to fruition what would be impossible for us with our limitations.

I hope that through what you are going to read you will hear God's invitation to participate in His work—impossible for you, but a piece of cake for Him.

May God surprise you by taking you through the experience of knowing Him more and better.

Injustice Reigns on Earth

Yes, injustice reigns on earth.

Am I saying something wrong? Am I wrong to make this comment?

A policeman had difficulty meeting the financial needs of his family. Some in his situation might have gotten involved with corruption and criminal activities, but he did not. Instead, he began to dedicate a few hours after his official shift to working as a security guard at a pizzeria. One day, several criminals entered the pizzeria, and he wanted to stop them. They emptied the cash register while one of the thieves pointed his gun at him. Once they got the money, the thief shot the policeman coldly in the head and withdrew.

That man was forty-three years old, and his death left a huge void in his family.

Does it seem unfair? Yes, it does. And there is much more injustice everywhere around you wherever you go.

Of course, I know that there are governments, laws, and institutions in charge of making sure everything works correctly. But even so, I argue that injustice reigns on earth.

Listen carefully to the news only once to confirm it. It can be enough that you pay attention to what is happening around you, that you listen to the complaints and comments of those who are victims of the abuse of others or are the object of the lies and violence that abound everywhere.

It may be enough if you to consider your own life. Almost all of us have experienced or are experiencing injustice in some area of our lives.

Injustice reigns on earth.

But this is not new, although apparently it has been increasing.

Why does all this happen? How can it be that we have advanced so much in the scientific field and we have developed so much at a technological level, but we cannot eradicate the injustice in our lives?

That's where some take the opportunity to rebuke God. I have heard them express their opinions with questions like "If there really is a God of love, why would He allow things like that to happen?"

And I answer: Are you really going to accuse God for the dispossession of the victims of injustice? Isn't it absolutely clear to you that all this is the result of the corruption that we all carry inside? Isn't it obvious that we all have a tendency to evil within us that often—in some cases more than in others—is externalized in horrific and devastating acts that are capable of ruining or destroying the lives of others? Don't you realize that we ourselves have closed the doors of our lives, our homes, and our institutions to God and then complain because He is not present to stop the injustice that we unleash ourselves?

And many times, unfortunately, pain results in more pain, and the victim ends up becoming a victimizer, and the cycle repeats itself, over and over again. Until when? Until when the voice that says "Enough!" is heard.

I am one of those who like to be aware of what is happening around them. The media we access today allow us to know not only the news but also the opinions of those who read or access them. Have you read the comments at the bottom of the news? It can be a very revealing experience. Do you know how most people react? Looking for a culprit; the government takes a good part of the blame, but there are also many others: the society, the economic system, the family of the criminals, the victim who looked for it in some way, the police who did not act when and how they should have, and many more.

What do you think? Have unfair situations occurred around you? If so, how do you react to them? Why do these things happen?

Maybe that's the key question: Why is all this happening?

It is obvious that there are no simple answers to this question, nor can it be generalized, because each case is different.

However, what I am going to do is invite you to look at a very old biblical story. Surprisingly for some, we will find in it points of contact with what happens to us here and now, and we will feel identified. The goal is that at the end, somehow (with the intervention of God, the Author of the Book), we may find healthy and edifying ways to face our own conflicts and the injustices with which we struggle in our own lives.

Ready? This is how the story begins:

> The people of Israel did what was evil in the sight of the LORD, and the LORD gave them into the hand of Midian seven years. And the hand of Midian overpowered Israel, and because of Midian the people of Israel made for themselves the dens that are in the mountains and the caves and the strongholds. For whenever the Israelites planted crops, the Midianites and the Amalekites and the people of the East would come up against them. They would encamp against them and devour the produce of the land, as far as Gaza, and leave no

sustenance in Israel and no sheep or ox or donkey. For they would come up with their livestock and their tents; they would come like locusts in number—both they and their camels could not be counted—so that they laid waste the land as they came in. (Judges 6:1–5)

I am convinced that the advance of injustice in the midst of human society is not something new. No, definitely, it's something that has been with us practically since the beginning. This old story makes it clear.

A PEOPLE IN TROUBLE

The story presents the situation of a people in trouble. The Israelites of the story are going through a bad time, one that affects them personally, their families, and their society, impeding the normal development of many aspects of their lives.

What happened to them? They were invaded by the Midianites, Amalekites, and other peoples of the East. As the story goes, the enemies arrived with their innumerable armies, who in turn traveled with the cattle they obtained after their multiple victories, and both them and their cattle devoured everything they found in their path. What they did not consume they trampled on, ruining the crops and leaving behind only poverty and devastation.

The Israelites could not continue with their lives normally. They even had to leave their own homes and settle in hiding places in the mountains and caves, and in other places where they could defend themselves.

Their lives were in danger, they had problems accessing the minimum resources to survive, they were scared; and the future looked absolutely uncertain.

I would like you to read that last sentence again. Haven't you been there? Although you may not have been part of a people that was invaded by the army of another nation, we have all experienced through limitations similar to those they faced.

I do not know what your economic situation is, but there are many on the planet who are experiencing difficulties – right now – to access the basic provisions to survive. Do you and your family have everything they need – food, implements for daily use, toiletries and cleaning, access to effective and trustworthy medical services? If you have all of that, you should thank God. But how about the rest?

Those Israelites lived in insecurity. Today, in our advanced society of the 21st century, people still live in insecurity. Many times, it is not the foreign armies that threaten us, but every day we hear of terrorist acts, unexpected aggressors, unnecessary violence. Yes, today too, many people experience fear, and fear for their own safety and that of their own.

They say that there were times when people and their families could be safe in a church. Do not take it for granted in our days.

It is assumed that schools are safe places. Are they?

Today there's many people for whom the future is something absolutely uncertain. Changes in society and the economy threaten the stability of many, and what was previously considered safe is no longer so. What can make the future uncertain? A disease can do it. The breakup of a marriage relationship can put everything in doubt. The loss of a job can make everything tremble.

Do you realize that beyond the historical differences that separate us from the protagonists of this biblical story, today we are exposed to challenges that could be compared with theirs?

Now, what was it that led them to that undesirable situation?

ARCHITECTS OF OUR OWN DESTINY

It may be somewhat shocking the direct way in which this story begins. Are you looking for responsible? The Bible presents them without filters.

> *The people of Israel did what was evil in the sight of the LORD …*

How long has it been since you listened to someone talking like this? Have you ever heard someone say, "This happened to me because I did something that offends the Lord"?

No, it's not a popular topic of conversation. Even when it could apply to many situations. This is a reference to a group of persons. With so many speculations that are made in search of the reasons why the economy, development, unemployment rate or other values of nations are wrong, you may never hear someone saying: "The fact is that we have been turning our backs towards God; we have offended Him with our actions."

It is evident that it is not popular to speak about sin. A big majority consider it an outdated, old-fashioned concept that no longer applies to human behavior.

But there is something that no one can deny: the actions of people bring consequences. What you do produces results.

The fact is that for one reason or another, although many avoid mentioning sin, we are all aware that our actions bring consequences. It is logical. If you throw a stone up it will be better you take cover, because the stone will fall down again; and if you recklessly stay out in the open, it can fall on top of you and hurt you.

But let's analyze this idea a little better.

Could it be that even today, offending the Lord, as this passage says, brings consequences on people?

If you are brave enough, do this brief exercise. Reread the first words of the passage we have just read, but in the place where the Israelites are mentioned, put the name of your family.

> *The* [your family name] ... *did what was evil in the sight of the LORD, and the LORD gave them into the hand of ...*

Or, if you prefer not to consider your family as a whole, consider how this sounds on a personal level, using the first person and placing your name in the place where the Israelites are mentioned:

> [Your name] ... *did what was evil in the sight of the LORD, and the LORD gave him into the hand of ...*

Do you recognize any moment in your life when you have done things that offended the Lord?

What consequences did that situation leave in your life?

Considering it more closely, we have to recognize that this concept of doing something that offends the Lord is based on two basic concepts:

1. God Cares About What People Do.

This is something that seems not to be in the minds of the majority. I mean, let us be honest: we all live life as it is presented to us, and we try to extract the best from it. We try to accumulate good experiences, and take advantage of everything good that we find in our path. And, to tell the truth, there are not many occasions in which we put ourselves to consider if what we do offends God or not. We think first of whether it benefits us or not, whether it does us good or not, whether we will have a good time or not. But if God likes it or offends Him ... No, it is not the thought that most have in mind when making their decisions.

Why do we ignore God in this way? Because we do not see Him, and because we prefer to pretend that He is not there, that He doesn't see what we are doing and does not know *why* we are doing it. Because we deceive ourselves thinking that nothing will happen if we act as if His commandments don't exist. Actually, isn't that what everyone does?

Many people would hide behind this question: "Does God care about people lives and what we do or do not do?" Whatever our answer to this question is, the truth is that the majority acts as if they consider that God cares nothing, as if it seems to them that God is not inclined to observe what is happening here and now.

But you know? It is not like this. God does care about our lives. Not only does he care: God is weighed by injustice, lies annoy Him and detests violence:

> *Woe to those who decree iniquitous decrees, and the writers who keep writing oppression, to turn aside the needy from justice and to rob the poor of my people of their right, that widows may be their spoil, and that they may make the fatherless their prey! What will you do on the day of punishment, in the ruin that will come from afar? To whom will you flee for help, and where will you leave your wealth?* (Isaiah 10:1 – 3)

> *Woe to those who devise wickedness and work evil on their beds! When the morning dawns, they perform it, because it is in the power of their hand. They covet fields and seize them, and houses, and take them away; they oppress a man and his house, a man and his*

inheritance. Therefore, thus says the LORD: behold, against this family I am devising disaster, from which you cannot remove your necks, and you shall not walk haughtily, for it will be a time of disaster. (Micah 2:1 – 3)

God is a righteous judge, and a God who feels indignation every day. (Psalms 7:11)

I could go on and on, filling pages with biblical passages that confirm the fact that God does not turn His eyes to the side when it comes to what happens between us humans. God sees us, and there are many – too many – times when He does not like what He sees at all.

Take it personally. God has seen, very clearly, what is happening and what has happened in your life. No, He wasn't looking the other way, and He hasn't been indifferent to those times when you have been treated with injustice.

God holds the position as the supreme Judge, as the One before whom we are all going to have to give an account of our actions and decisions.

And just as it is appointed for man to die once, and after that comes judgment, … (Hebrews 9:27)

God cares about what happens. That is why, at the time of that story, He clearly saw that people had turned their backs on Him and had acted "their own way", in open contradiction with His principles and purposes.

That brings us to the following point.

2. Universal Laws Do Exist.

We live in the world of relativism. According to the opinion of the majority, everything is relative – to each of us – and we can see it every day in the light of the tendencies that become popular in our time.

You may have already found yourself in some situation where two people – perhaps being one of them – discovered that they had different positions on a certain issue. They did not want to get involved in a pointless discussion, so they brought out that very popular version of respect, and someone said something like: "Okay, I do not agree, but I respect your position; Maybe it's fine for you, even if it's different for me."

I have seen different versions of this relative position. Some people have kindly congratulated me for my faith, encouraging me in the sense that it was fine for me, even though they had a totally different lifestyle and position. What was the idea behind their comments? That all "those things" do us good. Many think that all religious ideas and their practices do well, and that the results are all the same.

If that were true, there would be no universal truths, that is, laws or concepts that apply to all people, without exception. It would be the same to apply the laws of Islam, those of Catholicism, those of atheism or those of the satanic church. Is that so?

That statement (that the Israelites had done what offends the Lord) departs from the basis that there is a God in heaven, the Creator of everything that exists, including us, that has rules, laws, principles that should govern our existence according to His plan when He created us. What happens is that humans – fallen beings since we got away from Him, since we turned our backs on Him – often do what is offensive to Him.

Is what is offending God also done today?
Yes. And from there the consequences.

IF YOU LIGHT A FIRE, THERE WILL BE SMOKE

What happens when we act like this, turning a deaf ear to the will of God and taking charge of our lives "in our own way"?

It may happen what happened on that occasion:

> *… and the LORD gave them …*

This is where we would like to enjoy "the best of both worlds". We would like to do what we want with no consequences. We would like it to be possible to carry our "lucky cross" around our neck to protect us from all evil and danger, even if we do not take into account God's principles.

This is the word of warning that we have to keep in mind: what we do has consequences.

> *Do not be deceived: God is not mocked, for whatever one sows, that will he also reap. (Galatians 6: 7)*

Never better said. The consequences of our actions exist, and many times they hurt.

I don't know how many of the Israelites have immediately noticed the relationship between their estrangement from God and what was happening to them. Perhaps at first they did what most of us do today: They labeled the situation "disgraceful" and tried to get over it. But it wasn't that easy, so they had no choice but to think better of it.

Some here would stop to consider whether it would have been okay for God to hand them over to his enemies, as He did. Does this situation contradict the concept that God is love? What was God's intention in doing so? Did He want to hurt them, just for the sake of it?

No way. What God was doing was letting the weight of their own decisions fall on them, the consequences of the way they conducted themselves through life. But He did not do it with the intention of seeing them suffer or anything like it. God's intention, from the beginning, was for them to turn to Him, to get closer to Him, to regain the relationship they had with Him before that happened.

I want you to look at your own situation, your circumstances, through this very same perspective. God is working in your life, around you, and sometimes His most eloquent messages are not transmitted from the pulpit of a church but through the things that happen to you. Just as it happened on that occasion with the people of Israel.

What I want to ask you—what I think all of us have to do—is that you start paying close attention, because there are many occasions when God wants to speak to you through your circumstances. We need to begin to see God's intervention in what is happening in our lives and around us.

Sometimes it happens that you do what offends God, and sometimes God lets the weight of the consequences of your actions and decisions fall on you. He does not do it to sink you or to destroy you. On the contrary, although at first it may be difficult to understand, He does it because He loves you deeply, and because He wants to have you by His side, with all the privileges of His love and His grace.

Consider the aspects in which this situation affected the people of Israel when they offended God with their actions and lifestyle away from His principles.

1. They had to isolate themselves. *"...the people of Israel made for themselves the dens that are in the mountains and the caves and the strongholds"*. (Judges 6: 2).
2. They had to assume a defensive attitude. (Judges 6: 2).
3. They tried to overcome the situation, without success. *"For whenever the Israelites planted crops, the Midianites and the Amalekites and the people of the East would come up against them"*. (Judges 6: 3).
4. They faced severe financial problems. *"They would encamp against them and devour the produce of the land, as far as Gaza, and leave no sustenance in Israel and no sheep or ox or donkey. For they would come up with their livestock and their tents; they would come like locusts in number—both they and their camels could not be counted—so that they laid waste the land as they came in. And Israel was brought very low because of Midian"*. (Judges 6: 4-6).
5. They felt humiliated, defeated, and rejected.

Was it just what was happening to them? Was it fair for one or more foreign armies to come and unjustly take what had belonged to them, leaving them practically without sufficient resources for their survival?

No. It wasn't fair. They were being victims of the injustice that reigns on earth (since then).

Of course, that could have been our verdict if the passage had not started by pointing out that all of this happened as a consequence of the fact that the Israelites had offended God with their actions and their estrangement from Him.

Now think about this: We are looking at the story of something that happened a few thousand years ago, and yet we find people who saw their lives affected by problems in ways that we too regret and suffer. Yes, it is true that given the historical, social and technological differences that distinguish us from them, their problems seem much worse than the ones you and I face these days. Can you imagine if that happened to us and we had to go hiding in cold caverns without the comforts we are used to while we overcome our difficult circumstances? It would be terrible!

But saving the differences, it is possible that at some point in your life you have felt the need to separate yourself a bit from others while you put your thoughts in order to face your problems. If you are truly honest with yourself you will have to recognize that at different times in your life you have become defensive, probably to protect yourself from the hostile environment that surrounded you. Of course it was not as violent a hostility as the one the Israelites faced, but that hostility sure hurt, and you looked for ways to minimize the number of injuries you received.

Do I need to continue? People like you and I can feel identified with the rest too. Our economy can be shaken, in different ways and at different levels for everyone. You too have tried to overcome your problems, and sometimes you have not succeeded. Almost all of us have also gone through circumstances in which we have felt humiliated or rejected.

Do you remember all that?

Let God speak to you about it. He surely wants to do it.

Are you connecting the dots? Doesn't what happened to the people of Israel on that occasion set off some alarms within you? Can't it be that something similar happens to you (and maybe your family, yours)? I mean, you may have offended God with your actions and lifestyle, you may have turned away from Him, you may have turned your back on Him, and then you may have been faced with problems for which you saw no solution.

Do you realize that this is what happens to us many times? We too turn our backs on God! We also ignore Him or consider that there is no reason to give so much importance to His commandments and teachings! We also disconnect from Him by trying to live life "our way." After all, isn't that what everyone does?

How do we evaluate the situations that come our way? Consider how often we complain. Yes, many times we are overtaken by injustice. We think and usually come to the conclusion that this or that person, the government, the society, the economy are to blame. But what we do not usually recognize is that many times, even though there seems to be no connection between one thing and another, we receive nothing more than the consequences of our own actions.

The same God who dealt with those men and women on that occasion is the One who is relating with you today. Just as He did with them, God wants to get your attention. He delivered them into the hands of those enemies, and sometimes he has delivered you into the hands of the problems, the difficulties, the obstacles that have come your way in life. You know why? Because He loves you. Because He knows that ignoring Him and turning your back on Him only hurts you. Because He wants to give you the opportunity to cry out to Him, to seek Him with all your heart. God is speaking to you through what happens to you.

Just as He did with them.

That brings me to something that seems tremendously important to me. The account we are considering is part of the book of Judges. If you read it in full, you will find that the people of Israel repeat over and over the cycle of turning away from God and seeking Him. It is interesting that a statement that summarizes what is related in the book, appears precisely in its last verse:

> *In those days there was no king in Israel. Everyone did what was right in his own eyes.* (Judges 21:25)

Today we call it anarchy, and it is the same thing. Every time

I read the second part of this verse I feel like it is describing the time in which I live.

Yes, we all do. It is "normal" (because it is what everyone does). What do we do? What seems right in our own eyes. And since everybody lives the same way, it seems to us that it is not so bad.

But the truth is that it has consequences.

It is not unfair that this is the case. God has been warning us all along that it would be so, but we don't take Him seriously. So today God has you here, calling your attention, looking out before the mirror of His Word, so that you can reconsider your way of conducting yourself in life. Not everything that happens is your fault, but there are actions of yours that bring results.

Don't you think it would be good to personally re-analyze how you are managing your life?

It is not the end of the road. The recognition of our responsibility is the first step to receive the best news that have been announced in the entire history of mankind. Jesus Christ died in your place, bearing the consequences of your bad decisions.

But we need to start by taking our condition seriously, by taking responsibility for what we have not done well.

If you are taking this first step today, let God illuminate every corner of your existence. You may feel uncomfortable and embarrassed when it happens, but believe me, that becomes your best day, as it is the beginning of healing and restoration.

Take this path. There is restoration for you.

The Benefits of an Undesirable Moment

We all classify the different moments that we live in "good" and "bad".

For example you, meditate for a moment on your own life. What would you say have been the best moments (or the best times, the best experiences) of your life? And the worst? What have they been? Think about it for a moment.

This memory exercise can be very revealing. For most it is easier to recognize what have been the worst experiences of their lives. For some reason, our greatest regrets stand out and are easy to identify. But we have also had good times, and they have generated beautiful memories for us. For many, recalling times of joy is some kind of a refuge, a source of relief and energy to face the different circumstances that we have to live.

But have you ever thought that the things we live have a purpose, that things don't happen just because they do?

The fact of recognizing that the things that we live do not occur at random, that there is a purpose behind everything that happens, is not only an intellectual philosophical position, but it is something that leads us to position ourselves in front of every circumstance that comes our way with a different attitude.

It is not the same to stand in front of your house that is on fire only to lament the unfairness of such a situation, than to do it considering that there is something else, that there is still tomorrow, that there is a reason why that has happened, and that there is One who has the power to transform even the most painful experience into an epic victory.

But that attitude is decided by you, before everything happens.

That is why we are here, considering our good and bad times. Because there will be more of those, the bad and the good ones, and you and I need to be prepared for the next time we have to react to what happens to us.

So, how are you going to react the next time life presents you with some unwanted situation?

Actually, this is a trick question. Reactions are not planned; are produced. You cannot control your first reactions. What you can do is decide what to do once you stop to think about what is happening and you can develop, with a little more calm, an action plan to deal with your situation.

Consider if some of these are also your ways of reacting when something bad happens to you:

- **Anger.** For some, this is their most typical reaction. It is that way of facing circumstances by raising a fist in the air, mentioning all the reasons why what is happening is unfair and promising that someone will pay for that bad moment. You don't decide to get angry: you just get angry. But have you ever wondered what anger is? The truth is that anger is a psychological and physical resource that is triggered by the outbreak of adversity. It is an energy overload (in fact, during anger our adrenaline levels increase and we are able to double the strength we have in normal situations). But behind anger there is pain. Every single time. You get angry because something hurt you, something let you bleeding inside, something broke your heart. And if you let anger control your words, your actions, and your decisions, you will end up doing what you will later regret. I imagine you don't want to let anger get the better of you.

- **Isolation.** There are those who react to adversity by shutting themselves up. It is as if you sit on the ground in a ball, as if you are trying to invoke some kind of protective shield that surrounds you and protects you from what could hurt you. If you are not one of the people who react this way to problems, you will surely identify those who do. When difficulties arise, they move away from others, they are not available for communication, they do not participate in their regular activities. Does that fix the problem? No. It is just a way to cope or process the situation.

- **Sadness.** You might as well ask me if this is a reaction. Of course we all get sad when something hurts us. Both those who get angry and those who isolate themselves experience sadness as part of the "package" that accompanies the undesirable situation. But some people seem to cling to sadness more than others. It is as if they stopped there, affected by that destructive emotion, unable to participate in laughter and song, as if holding on to that time of darkness that falls like a cloak over their souls. It is in this situation that some people can lean towards depression, that persistent cloak of darkness so difficult to shake off. In some cases, this stagnation in sadness can be related to self-pity, that position in which one regrets what happens to him or her and feels sorry for himself or herself.

- **Search for solutions.** I think we all look for solutions when something goes wrong. Some, however, react immediately and almost instinctively in search of them. Instead of spending time dwelling on anger, loneliness, or sadness, you can strive to find the way out, to find a way to overcome the problem. You can say that this option is a good thing, for rather than let circumstances leave us frozen it moves us productively toward what lies ahead. The problem, sometimes, is that we may get to move like a swimmer in trouble looking for *any* kind of solution. The truth is that not all pieces of advise or ideas to face a situation are good, and we need to learn to distinguish the difference between the bad and the good ones.

- **Search for culprits.** This is another natural and typical way of reacting when faced with difficulty: you immediately start to consider who to blame for what happened. This reaction can be related to that of anger, because you look for the culprit and then take charge of venting your anger on that person, and this can happen in different ways. Faced with this reaction, you could well ask yourself: What do I solve with my accusations? It can be a very emotional but impractical way to deal with difficult circumstances.

- **Search for allies.** I think you can also recognize that this is something we all do: we realize that we are in trouble, we assume the damage that the situation is causing, and then we look around, wondering who can help us overcome the obstacle. This is or can be very revealing, because it tends to let us know who really care about us and who is willing to extend a hand if necessary. At the same time, it is good that we bear in mind that not all allies are good company. The cost of some favors can be high, depending on who is the person we turn to. Not all likely helpers will get us on the right track once the difficulty is overcame. Remember that when you turn to someone for help, you establish a bond of trust with that person that lasts beyond the test.

So it would be interesting for you to start thinking about your own life, how you react to difficulty. What do you do most often when you find yourself in trouble? Do you get angry? Do you start looking for someone to accuse? Do you sink into anguish? Do you rush off looking for the first solution to appear - whatever it is?

You know? It is good that you take some time to consider all this, especially if right now you are not experiencing a time when problems consume your energy, your time and your thoughts. The moment of the fight will come, and it will be good that you already have a strategy, that you already know how you will deliberately face the path to the solution.

Now, talking about difficulties, reactions and solutions, where is God and your relationship with Him at the moment of facing the difficulty?

Have you noticed that God often allows things to happen to us that sadden us, confuse us, or hurt us?

It sounds a bit strong, but it happens. Have you ever wondered why it happens? That is, those of us who believe in Jesus know that we have been reconciled to God. Furthermore, the Word of God contains promises that assure us that God is on our side, that He is our Defender and Protector, our High Refuge. So how does God allow these things that confuse and worry us to happen to us?

Would you understand if I told you that God allows all this because He loves us?

Think for a moment about your problems, your difficulties, those complicated moments that you have had to face in your life. You know? God allowed them because He loves you.

We need to understand this: God understands perfectly what is best for our lives, much better than ourselves. We can ask ourselves a hundred million times how our difficulties are the best, but we need to trust that God knows what He is doing.

Consider for a moment what happened to the people of Israel

on that occasion when they were facing the invasion of their enemies.

> *The people of Israel did what was evil in the sight of the Lord, and the Lord gave them into the hand of Midian seven years. And the hand of Midian overpowered Israel, and because of Midian the people of Israel made for themselves the dens that are in the mountains and the caves and the strongholds. For whenever the Israelites planted crops, the Midianites and the Amalekites and the people of the East would come up against them. They would encamp against them and devour the produce of the land, as far as Gaza, and leave no sustenance in Israel and no sheep or ox or donkey. For they would come up with their livestock and their tents; they would come like locusts in number—both they and their camels could not be counted—so that they laid waste the land as they came in. And Israel was brought very low because of Midian. And the people of Israel cried out for help to the Lord. When the people of Israel cried out to the Lord on account of the Midianites, …* (Judges 6:1 - 7)

We have already considered the situation of the people of Israel on that occasion. They had offended God with their actions and their lifestyle contrary to His values, and God had allowed their enemies to get the better of them. Here it clearly says that *God gave them into the hands* of their enemies.

Why would God do that? Didn't God love His people?

Of course He loved them! And precisely because He loved them, He allowed them to face those difficult circumstances. God wanted to bring them just to the point where they had to turn to Him.

God wanted them to cry out to Him.

We will consider later what happened after they cried out, but I consider that this point, this moment in which they recognize their need for God's intervention in their lives, is radically important.

Just as it is for your life and mine.

The reality is this: During times of peace and prosperity we are tempted to look away from God. We relax, we settle in while we enjoy the good time and in different ways we stop giving God His rightful place in our lives.

You and I were not created to live apart from God. Our lives take on meaning and are placed where they need to be when we experience a vibrant and active relationship with our Creator.

Sometimes we misunderstand love. We can conclude that love consists in God approving and applauding everything we do, even if what we do offends Him and leads us away from Him. But God is a responsible and loving Father, and sometimes He will use discipline and firmness to get us back on track, knowing what is really good for us.

God allowed the enemies to attack Israel to hear the voice of His children again, to bless them with His answers and His presence, to protect them with His direction and care. This is what love looks like.

God wants to hear your voice again. God knows that when you are apart from Him you hurt yourself and expose yourself to the lies, violence and injustice of this world. That is why sometimes He will allow difficult circumstances to come into your life, because when you experience them you will return to Him.

You will cry out.

God wants to hear your cry.

Do you know what it is to cry out to God? The cry is not one of our usual prayers, the kind we raise to God to give thanks for food. Crying out is another form of expression.

We could compare this cry out with the exclamations that come out of our mouth when something hurts us. I imagine that at least once you have hit your little toe when you tripped over something or slammed your finger on a door. How painful! And just when you felt the pain you uttered an exclamation that came out of your mouth without having been planned: "Ouch!" (that's the short version). The cry, as a way of raising our prayer to God, is something similar. It is our way of communicating with Him when something hurts, saddens us, worries us, when life hits us. The cry can be accompanied by tears, screams, sighs, silences and deep emotions.

It is the voice of our despair. It is our cry for help.

It is our recognition that we desperately need God, that we need His help, and that we cannot live without Him.

In the Word of the Lord we can find this situation many times. This story of the Israelites oppressed by the Midianites is not the only time the cry is mentioned. When you go through the pages of the book of Psalms, for example, you will find the cry and the testimony of what happened when they cried out from several of their authors.

One of the favorite promises of many Christians is this:

> *Thus says the Lord who made the earth, the Lord who formed it to establish it—the Lord is his name: Call to me and I will answer you, and will tell you great and hidden things that you have not known.*(Jer . 33: 2, 3)

God spoke these words to Jeremiah in a time of great difficulty, both for him personally and for the city of Jerusalem where he was. The one who makes the promise presents Himself full of authority, worthy, powerful, the Creator of all that exists. The difficulties they faced at that time had not diminished the power and authority of God in the least.

The same thing happens in your life. God is no less powerful when you face difficulties. Problems are not a sign that God has become weak or distracted. God continues to know what He is doing even though we don't understand it, and He continues to work for our good.

When we cry out to God we are ready to receive this promise. God declares in His Word that when we cry out to Him He will respond, and not only that, but He will open our eyes and our hearts so that we understand what until that moment we had not understood.

We need to recognize that there are many things that we do not know, many that we do not understand or know. But God does know them, and He wants to reveal them to us, so that we learn and grow, knowing Him.

God wants to give you more than what you have received until now, He wants you to understand what has been hidden from your eyes until today.

Do you remember these words of Job?

> *I had heard of you by the hearing of the ear, but now my eye sees you; ...* (Job 42: 5)

Job was in trouble, and he faced great pain. He cried out to God (we could say that much of his book is the content of his cry) and God answered him, and showed him what he had not even been able to imagine before: God himself made Himself known to him.

God wants to take you to a new level of knowledge of His person, and He wants to open your heart so that you are able to understand what until now you could not. You just need to trust Him and seek Him with all your heart. Cry out to Him.

There is one Psalm in particular that I regard as powerful testimony to the power of the cry in the life of the believer. Read these words very carefully:

<blockquote>

1 Oh give thanks to the Lord, for he is good,
for his steadfast love endures forever!

2 Let the redeemed of the Lord say so,
whom he has redeemed from trouble

3 and gathered in from the lands,
from the east and from the west,
from the north and from the south.

4 Some wandered in desert wastes,
finding no way to a city to dwell in;

5 hungry and thirsty,
their soul fainted within them.

6 Then they cried to the Lord in their trouble,
and he delivered them from their distress.

7 He led them by a straight way
till they reached a city to dwell in.

8 Let them thank the Lord for his steadfast love,
for his wondrous works to the children of man!

9 For he satisfies the longing soul,
and the hungry soul he fills with good things.

10 Some sat in darkness and in the shadow of death,
prisoners in affliction and in irons,

11 for they had rebelled against the words of God,
and spurned the counsel of the Most High.

12 So he bowed their hearts down with hard labor;
they fell down, with none to help.

</blockquote>

13 Then they cried to the Lord in their trouble,
    and he delivered them from their distress.
14 He brought them out of darkness and the
    shadow of death,
    and burst their bonds apart.
15 Let them thank the Lord for his steadfast love,
    for his wondrous works to the children of man!
16 For he shatters the doors of bronze
    and cuts in two the bars of iron.
17 Some were fools through their sinful ways,
    and because of their iniquities suffered affliction;
18 they loathed any kind of food,
    and they drew near to the gates of death.
19 Then they cried to the Lord in their trouble,
    and he delivered them from their distress.
20 He sent out his word and healed them,
    and delivered them from their destruction.
21 Let them thank the Lord for his steadfast love,
    for his wondrous works to the children of man!
22 And let them offer sacrifices of thanksgiving,
    and tell of his deeds in songs of joy!
23 Some went down to the sea in ships,
    doing business on the great waters;
24 they saw the deeds of the Lord,
    his wondrous works in the deep.
25 For he commanded and raised the stormy wind,
    which lifted up the waves of the sea.
26 They mounted up to heaven; they went down
    to the depths;
    their courage melted away in their evil plight;
27 they reeled and staggered like drunken men

and were at their wits' end.

28 Then they cried to the Lord in their trouble,
and he delivered them from their distress.
29 He made the storm be still,
and the waves of the sea were hushed.
30 Then they were glad that the waters were quiet,
and he brought them to their desired haven.
31 Let them thank the Lord for his steadfast love,
for his wondrous works to the children of man!

(Psalms 107:1 - 31)

To some it might seem like a long passage, but for me it is worthy. How many times have I felt identified with these words! Don't you?

This is the Psalm of those who cry out to God. This is our testimony, that of those of us who have searched for God with desperation, with hunger and thirst for His presence, without understanding the reasons for what was happening, but knowing that He was listening and had promised to respond.

In the Psalm we find the testimonies (situations) of different people who came face to face with difficulty and pain. In some cases—although we need to keep in mind that it is not in all—the problems that these people faced were, as also happened with the people of Israel in the story that is related in Judges 6, a consequence of their bad decisions that kept them away from God. Perhaps they have thought, said or considered, as we do so many times, that nothing was going to happen, that there would be no great consequences if one strayed "a little" from God's teachings. Then they were caught up in the storm of difficulty and had to recognize that only in God is there peace, wisdom, comfort, and strength.

Then they cried to the Lord in their trouble,
and he delivered them from their distress.

Then they cried to the Lord in their trouble,
and he delivered them from their distress.

Then they cried to the Lord in their trouble,
and he delivered them from their distress.

Then they cried to the Lord in their trouble,
and he delivered them from their distress. (verses 6, 13, 19, 28)

Do you know what these words teach us? That the cry to God does work! That God is there to listen and respond, to reach out as we turn to Him.

Reread Psalm 107. With which of the situations do you feel identified? Which of them can represent any of the struggles you have faced or are facing in your life?

Have you felt lost, disoriented, not knowing what to do?

Do you walk as if you are chained, surrounded by darkness and no human help is enough?

Has the disease caught up with you and your situation fills you with anguish?

Do you feel as if everything around you is a huge and powerful storm that you cannot get out of? Do you feel as if you are stumbling without finding answers?

Cry out to God!

God, who revealed Himself to us through Jesus, who showed us His eternal love by giving His only Son to forgive our sins and give us eternal life, is longing to hear your voice. Your own soul desperately needs that moment when you cry out with your voice seeking His presence and His work.

Do not settle for reading these words. They don't make any sense if you don't respond to them by seeking God with all your heart. If this is not your time of difficulty, do not wait until you are in the middle of the storm to start cultivating a close relationship with God.

Don't look around for someone who can pray for you. Yes, God hears and answers the prayer of others too, but He wants to hear your voice. God does not answer to church leaders more than to you. His power is not greater when someone else prays. God wants to show you all His greatness and love as an answer to *your prayer*. So cry out to Him!

1. He who cries out is in trouble.
2. The person crying out acknowledges that he/she cannot overcome the situation on his/her own and that needs help.
3. Those crying out recognize that God has power to help them.
4. Many times, God allows our difficult circumstances to draw us closer to Him.

Trust. God has not lost control. He wants you to meet Him, and He is capable of transforming what seems like a final defeat into the greatest of your victories.

Cry out to God!

Take it Seriously

T here are things we take seriously, others we don't.
It is something we all do.

If you are approached by a seven-feet-tall person with a covered face and a firearm pointed at you, you will feel more than intimidated. You will put aside all your other thoughts and focus on what is happening to you at that moment. You will feel the impact of fear drowning out your emotions and almost instinctively you will raise your hands so that the person does not feel threatened in any way, in an attempt to minimize the possibility that he will shoot you. At that moment you will be willing to give everything you have with you, if the person asks you to. It is logical, you will tell me, that you take the threat that this person poses to you very seriously. Yes, you will take it very seriously.

But what would your reaction be if a girl of about four years old appears in front of you pointing her toy revolver at you? Oh well, that would be different, don't you think? Of course. In that case, you would probably immediately smile, and perhaps even become spontaneously playful, pretending that the girl hit you with one of her shots, or perhaps you may place your own fingers as if they were also weapons, in case you have to defend yourself before this surprise attack. There will be no adrenaline or spontaneous prayers motivated by fear, but smiles, relaxation, and some nice comment to make the child smile. With all due respect to the minor, but you won't take her seriously. It does not pose a threat to you. No, you won't take her seriously.

The same happens with many of the situations in our life. There are so many values and circumstances that we handle during our existence, that we somehow classify them, usually without trying, according to their importance to us.

Thus, there are things in your life that you take seriously, and others that you don't.

Sometimes we are so busy and fast-paced living our lives, meeting our commitments, nurturing our relationships, and taking care of ourselves and those we love that we don't devote much of our thoughts to this. But since we are talking about what is or is not important to us, I would like to propose that you answer this question for yourself:

Are you taking the really important things seriously?

Do you know why I ask you this? Because I have discovered that sometimes we can be wrong. It may happen that, perhaps because of the speed at which we live and the speed with which we make decisions, we overlook things that are truly important, and to which we perhaps do not recognize the value.

It may be that you are not taking seriously something that should be a priority for you.

What if you think about it? Analyze it in your heart as we consider this part of the story of the people of Israel. At some point, they also did not take seriously what was vitally important to their lives.

When the people of Israel cried out to the Lord on account of the Midianites, the Lord sent a prophet to the people of Israel. And he said to them, "Thus says the Lord, the God of Israel: I led you up from Egypt and brought you out of the house of slavery. And I delivered you from the hand of the Egyptians and from the hand of all who oppressed you, and drove them out before you and gave you their land. And I said to you, 'I am the Lord your God; you shall not fear the gods of the Amorites in whose land you dwell.' But you have not obeyed my voice." (Judges 6.7–10, ESV)

Let's take a moment to remember what was happening in the life of Israel as a nation at that time. They were in trouble. They had economic, social, cultural problems, and of all kinds. Why? Because their enemies were more powerful than them, they had very numerous armies with them that invaded their territory, consumed their resources and destroyed their crops. They were being victims of violence and abuse from their enemies.

It was in those circumstances that they cried out to God. In the verse before what we just read, it says this:

And Israel was brought very low because of Midian.
And the people of Israel cried out for help to the Lord.
(Judges 6: 6)

When they perceived that their problems were beyond them, they cried out to God. They didn't just pray; *they cried out* . They were at the end of the rope, and they probably feared that this would continue until they ceased to exist. Then they *cried out* to God for His help.

It is possible that it has happened to you too, that you have had to face difficult circumstances in which you reached that level of despair in which you cry out to God with all your heart, with anguish, with the hope that God will intervene to put an end to the overwhelming weight of difficulty.

When You Receive What You Are Not Asking For

If you've been there, in a situation like that, it is certain that what you expected and hoped was that God would intervene immediately, concluding the problem, manifesting the instant solution that will put an end to the times of worry and pain.

I am convinced that this is what the people of Israel expected to happen when they cried out to God out of their anguish. They felt that they couldn't take it anymore, they lacked solutions, and they hoped that God would show up right then, without delay, to free them from oppression.

And indeed, God could do it. God could have sent the army of another nation more powerful than the Midianites to defeat them or put them to flight and then go elsewhere to continue conquering, leaving Israel free of its problems. He could have sent a plague, an earthquake, a large hail shower to defeat that powerful invading army. He could have done it, of course.

But He did not.

Instead, He did something else.

Most people find it annoying if they ask for something and receive something different . It is something that has happened to us since we were children. Imagine the boy who asked for his favorite toy for his birthday, but his mom gives him another gift instead. There may be children who take it well or who understand that they will have their request some other time, but many of the little infants can throw a long tantrum because they did not receive what they had asked for or expected. And they may have already understood that their crying has the ability to produce changes in the mood and decisions of their elders, so they will express it with intensity.

Something similar, but when we are older can happen when we are at a restaurant. Wouldn't it be tremendously frustrating and disrespectful if when they bring us the food it turns out that it is not what we ordered? There are those who would get angry and raise their voices to claim what they asked for in the first place. And an apology.

Furthermore, on that occasion the people of Israel were in trouble, and they had cried out to God for His intervention to help them overcome the complicated situation they were in. They weren't asking to be indulged or to receive a random favor. They had real problems, and they needed urgent solutions.

It was then that they experienced that God, on many occasions, does not do things our way, but His way. He is God, and He really knows what is really good for us, even if we, at a certain moment, see it differently.

God did not send them an army; He sent a messenger.

Has something similar ever happened to you?

If at this moment you do not identify any experience in which something like that has happened, even so, please think about it. This can happen to you.

Prayer is a wonderful resource, the most powerful we have. The simple fact of being able to use our voice and our words to communicate with our Creator, knowing that He listens to us and that He promised to answer us, is amazing. But it is in prayer that we discover, perhaps more clearly than in any other moment, that God does not do things *as we see fit*.

Another aspect to consider is the right time. Sometimes we ask for something feeling we need it so badly that it has to arrive *now*, *without delay*. But God's timing may be different. It may happen that being in the heat of battle we fail to understand the benefit of the apparent delay in God's response, but we need to learn to trust, because He *really* knows what is best.

PAUSE AND CONSIDER

We are people of action. Well, at least most are. When we do something, and especially when we *need* something, we don't usually take breaks or stop. We try to get straight to the point, through the shortest possible path to resolving the situation.

But, I suppose you've noticed in this story, God sometimes calls us to pause. God wants us to make the best of the situations we face. Our circumstances are not just "things that happen", events that have happened to us by coincidence, "things in life." Everything we live has a purpose, and there is something we need to learn in every moment of our lives.

I know this is not something you do in every situation you face. Neither do I. But we need to learn that we are relating with God, that the Father seeks to get our attention, and that we don't have to ignore Him.

That is what God did when the Israelites cried out for His help in the difficult circumstances they faced. He called them to pause and consider their spiritual situation.

This is a truth that I think we need to assume:

God wants you to know what your spiritual condition is.

Most people settle for evaluating the material aspects of what they experience. Are they healthy? Do they have a plate of food on the table? Do they have money in their bank account? Do they have someone to spend some quality time with? If the answers to these more or less superficial questions are yes, then, why bother? "Life is one and you have to enjoy it," they would say. And they try to do that, without pausing, without taking seriously their own spiritual situation, even if God calls their attention and tries to make them reason about the path they are traveling on.

Please don't do the same. If God is calling your attention at this time, stop, relate with God, learn what He wants to teach you, get to know Him and listen to His voice.

That was what God wanted to do before responding by providing for the needs of His people.

So God, when the people cried out for His help, sent them a prophet. And what did the prophet have to tell them?

1. Reconsider Who God Is

The words were recorded with a high degree of accuracy. The prophet said:

> *"Thus says the Lord, the God of Israel ..."*

Wait, don't pass up this introduction to God's message as if it were nothing more than that. These words mean something.

That humble and anonymous prophet (the name of God's messenger is not even mentioned) fulfilled his mission of transmitting the words of the Almighty, beginning as did the rest of the Old Testament prophets. He began by saying *"Thus says the Lord."*

That shouldn't be too surprising. That man was clarifying that what he was going to tell them was not his own opinion about what was happening, but that he was communicating the Word of God, the message of the Creator. But exactly below he made one more clarification:

> *… God of Israel.*

These words are something like God's signature at the bottom of the message that was about to be communicated. The One who sent these words was the God of Israel Himself.

God's children had cried out for His help, and He was answering them. He does so by making it clear who it is that speaks to them, the *I Am*, the God of the people of Israel. For them, this introduction had a very important meaning. The one speaking to them was not only "God", but was *their* God.

The Israelites knew very well that the surrounding nations worshiped other gods, had their idols, and honored numerous deities. But the one who addressed them, the one to whom they cried out, was *their* God, the God of Israel.

This is not a recognition of the existence of other valid or comparable gods with God.

> *It was not because you were more in number than any other people that the Lord set his love on you and chose you, for you were the fewest of all peoples, but it is because the Lord loves you and is keeping the oath that he swore to your fathers, that the Lord has brought you out with a mighty hand and redeemed you from the house of slavery, from the hand of Pharaoh king of Egypt. Know therefore that the Lord your God is God, the faithful God who keeps covenant and steadfast love with those who love him and keep his commandments, to a thousand generations …* (Deuteronomy 7: 7 - 9)

Is it clear to you? The Great I Am is the only true God, the Creator, faithful God. God wanted His children to know that He was speaking to them.

At the same time, the fact that He introduced Himself as the God of Israel was a reminder of the covenant. God had made a covenant with the people of Israel, a covenant on which all His promises rested and which made the relationship between Him and the Israelites different from His relationship with any other people.

> *I will take you to be my people, and I will be your God, and you shall know that I am the Lord your God, who has brought you out from under the burdens of the Egyptians.* (Exodus 6: 7)

> *And I will walk among you and will be your God, and you shall be my people.* (Leviticus 26:12)

It was not "just any God" who addressed Israel with those words: it was *their* God. There was a covenant between them, and God was faithful to that covenant.

The people of Israel had been unfaithful to that covenant, but God did not consider it invalid. He was still faithful to that pact, and when He spoke to them He reminded them that covenant.

Israel repeatedly demonstrated its ability to break God's covenant, failing time and time again. That is why there came a time when God made a very solemn promise, which affects us:

> *"Behold, the days are coming, declares the Lord, when I will make a new covenant with the house of Israel and the house of Judah, not like the covenant that I made with their fathers on the day when I took them by the hand to bring them out of the land of Egypt, my*

covenant that they broke, though I was their husband, declares the Lord. For this is the covenant that I will make with the house of Israel after those days, declares the Lord: I will put my law within them, and I will write it on their hearts. And I will be their God, and they shall be my people. And no longer shall each one teach his neighbor and each his brother, saying, 'Know the Lord,' for they shall all know me, from the least of them to the greatest, declares the Lord. For I will forgive their iniquity, and I will remember their sin no more." (Jer . 31:31 - 34)

These words find perfect fulfillment through the work, sacrifice, and resurrection of Jesus Christ for us. God never stopped intending to be *our* God. Through Jesus, God extended this covenant relationship with Him so that all of us who believe in Jesus would get to be *His children.*

I think all of us need to pause, even as we consider the urgency of our problems and our need for solutions, to turn to God, to get closer to the God who made that covenant with us on the cross, when Jesus shed His blood for us.

Just like the Israelites at that time, those of us who believe in Jesus also have a special relationship with God, and He introduces Himself to us, as well as to them, as *our* God. If you believe in Jesus Christ, you need to hear the voice of *your* God. God is no longer simply "God" for you, but is *Immanuel* (God with us), and as our Savior taught us well, He is our *Father* . Yes, God is not simply "God" to us, a spiritual entity disconnected from our lives, our needs, our performance. God is *our* God, the Father.

2. Let's Remember What God Already Did.

So you cried out to God. Well done! God will answer. But it would be good for you to remember that this is not the first time you relate with God, this is not the first time that God intervenes in your life. Reconsider your story and remember: God has been there before.

That is what God did to Israel when they cried out to Him. He made them remember.

> *And I delivered you from the hand of the Egyptians*
> *and from the hand of all who oppressed you, and drove*
> *them out before you and gave you their land.*

No, this was not the first time that the people of Israel had a relationship with God. There was a whole history, lived experiences, victories obtained, in which God had intervened on their behalf. When His people cried out to Him, God took the opportunity to remind them of what He had done for them before. Those people had much to celebrate because of their relationship with God. They had been chosen from all other nations as God's people, they had been rescued from slavery when they were oppressed in Egypt, they had been given a land from which God Himself expelled its oppressors. Yes, they had a lot to thank God for.

Now, this is also a wake-up call for us who now cry out to God. Yes, thank God who hears and answers our prayers, but please don't forget who God is and what He has done for you!

I would like to ask you a favor that I consider very important to you: before reading further, take some time to answer this question:

What would God say (or says) when you cry out to Him at this time and He turns to you to remind you of what He has done in your life at other times? Take some time to remember how God intervened in your life in the past. Yes, now.

There is no doubt that all of us who believe in Jesus have a lot to thank God for. At some point we were blind, like everyone else, being ignorant of God's love, grace, and power.

> *And you were dead in the trespasses and sins in which you once walked, following the course of this world, following the prince of the power of the air, the spirit that is now at work in the sons of disobedience— among whom we all once lived in the passions of our flesh, carrying out the desires of the body and the mind, and were by nature children of wrath, like the rest of mankind.* (Ephesians 2: 1 - 3)

Don't forget, please don't forget what God did for you. God did not want His people to forget what He had done for them, nor does He want us today to forget the immense work He has done to save us, to open our eyes to the salvation that is in Jesus Christ, to forgive our sins, to renew our hope, to reconcile us with Him, to put peace in our hearts.

No. God doesn't want you to forget.

Even more, God wants you to keep it in mind each of your days.

And it's not just about what He did to save us. This is surely not the first time you have cried out to God for help. Throughout our lives, Christians are adding experiences in which God's intervention has been vital for us to move forward. What have we learned from those experiences? What have the prayers God answered us in the past taught us?

The same God who showed you the power of the cross for

your salvation is the One who comes to answer you today. The same God who heard and answered your prayer when you were in trouble, when your heart was broken under the weight of circumstances in the past, is the one who is also attentive to your prayer today.

Each of our experiences, when we recognize God's intervention in our lives, should have the capacity of feeding our faith. God is going to approach us to face this reality: "Do you understand why you know that I have the power to help you in the midst of your circumstances? Because I already did it before, because I was there when you needed me, because I answered your prayer in the midst of your brokenness and made a covenant with you through the blood of Jesus".

Do you recognize the value of what God has already done in you?

Let the way God has already revealed Himself to you in the past renew your faith for what you have to face today and for what lies ahead.

> *Jesus Christ is the same yesterday and today and forever.* (Hebrews 13: 8)

3. Let's Remember What God Has Taught Us.

God definitely doesn't want us to forget who He is and what He has done in our lives. That was true for the Israelites attacked and oppressed by the Midianites many centuries ago and it is also true for you and me at this time.

But the Father not only wants us to remember what He has done, but also to take into account what He has taught us.

Before the oppression of the Midianites and neighboring nations occurred, the people of Israel had received much teaching from God. Most people remember the Ten Commandments, but not everyone takes into account that those ten are immersed in a much larger body of teachings, in what the Israelites knew as the Law, that had been revealed through Moses.

Yes, the Law had been revealed to the people of Israel. The story and content is basically found in the book of Exodus (there are also laws in Leviticus and Numbers). It is interesting to remember that when the people (the new generations) were about to enter the Promised Land after the pilgrimage in the desert, God reminded them of the teachings of the law, and that is the content of the book of Deuteronomy. It was also Moses' last ministerial assignment before his passing.

We have already said that God wants us to remember. But He does not want us to remember only the events: He wants us to remember His words.

On that occasion, He said to the people of Israel:

> *And I said to you, 'I am the Lord your God; you shall not fear the gods of the Amorites in whose land you dwell.'*

Just as He did with the people of Israel back then, God has taught you things too. It may sound a bit strange to some that someone says "God taught me" or "God told me", but the disciples of Jesus are people who listen to the voice of God. Yes, as it sounds. We are people who have listened to the voice of God and have been taught by Him.

Christians have established a personal and deep relationship with God. To begin with, that relationship began because His Spirit convinced us of our spiritually bankrupt condition when we were without Jesus, and it was then that we began to hear His voice. It was He who showed us the importance of Jesus and His power to save us, and thanks to that we believed and received eternal life. From then on we walk hand in hand with Him, we try to act constantly according to His will, we go through life listening to His voice.

If you are a child of God because you have believed in Jesus, then you have heard the voice of God, and probably every day God is teaching you something new.

Then, God can bring to your memory His word, just as He could tell the Israelites on that occasion that He had already told them His truth.

What things has God told you?

They have all been for your good. God has been speaking and teaching you so that you can live in His will, according to the purposes for which He created you.

Do you recall what God has been teaching you?

God has used the Bible to speak to your heart. He used the church, the Bible studies, the messages you heard, the Christian music. He clarified your understanding with His Word and continues to do so every day, because while we are in this life we are not able to understand everything clearly, until we are in His presence.

How do you think God would complete the phrase "I told you ..." for you?

There are times when, even having listened to the voice of God and having learned from Him, we have not acted according to His principles.

4. Let's Acknowledge Our Mistakes.

This is a difficult step. It is not easy for us to admit our mistakes.

This is something that has happened since the beginning of human history. When God called Adam's attention to having eaten the fruit of the tree of the knowledge of good and evil, something that He had forbidden, Adam exclaimed:

> *"The woman whom you gave to be with me, she gave me fruit of the tree, and I ate."* (Genesis 3:12)

That's how quickly humans learned to transfer our responsibility for a bad decision.

But you don't need to open the Bible to see this. It is enough for you to look at a little boy when his mother arrives and discovers that he smeared the whole place with paint. He will immediately look up to accuse his brother as responsible, even though the two of them had been doing it together, not caring about whether it was okay or not.

No, it is not easy for us to recognize that we have taken the wrong path, that we have not done things well, that we have ignored the wise teachings that have been transmitted to us.

But it is vitally important that we do so.

That is why God came to reproach those Israelites:

> *But you have not obeyed my voice.*

God had sent a messenger to remind them of who He was, that they had a covenant with Him, that this was not the first time He had intervened in their lives to bless them, and that He had taught them how to live according to His will. God reminded them of specific commands He had given them regarding not imitating the religious and spiritual conduct of their neighbors. Then He tells them what they already knew, even if they preferred not to say it: they had not obeyed God's teaching.

The reality that God was referring to was that the Israelites had indeed worshiped the gods of the neighboring nations. They had considered that it should not be something so important or so bad, since the others did it and apparently nothing bad happened to them. They had not taken seriously the Word of God, which was important, and had acted in their own way. And now God was confronting them with that reality. Right here is the irony: when they were in trouble they cried out to God, not to the alien gods they had been worshiping. They knew who the true God was. God was not going to help them without facing their spiritual reality. Sin had driven them away from Him.

God is immensely good, and He always works to bless us, care for us, and guide us. There are many occasions when God does not let the consequences of our bad decisions fall on us. But there are times when He does. Why? Does He do it just so He can say that He was always right and we were wrong? Even if He did it with that intention, it would be justified. But no, He does not do it just to demonstrate the greatness of His wisdom; He does it to get us up once more, to restore us to a perfect relationship with Him, to get us back on track, so that we don't miss out on all that He has in store for us.

Before sending His help, God wanted His children to recognize their spiritual condition, and that they could assume in front of Him that they had turned their back on Him, that once again they had tried to live in their own way, without taking into account His principles, teachings and commandments.

God wanted them to understand what their spiritual condition was.

You don't have to be too smart to understand that God wants to do the same to us. God wants to help you recognize what your own spiritual situation is. We are not going to say that everything that happens to us is the direct consequence of our bad decisions, but it is something that happens many times.

God doesn't want to just take you out of the difficult circumstances we face. He wants to do it, yes, but He also wants the same situation to teach you, to take advantage of the experience to obtain the best and grow spiritually, in the relationship with Him and in His knowledge.

Don't you think it would be good for you to analyze your life, to meditate deeply on what God has been teaching you and how you applied His teachings or the fact that you did not apply them?

> *Search me, O God, and know my heart! Try me and know my thoughts! And see if there be any grievous way in me, and lead me in the way everlasting!* (Psalm 139: 23, 24)

This is how David prayed as he recognized the perfect way in which God knew him, without limitations. Don't you think that this would also be the way in which we too could come before God today?

> *My Lord, help me understand my own spiritual condition! I'm willing to let you reveal even my most embarrassing mistakes. I want to understand, good Father, so that I can return to the right path, so that everything that may be an obstacle to my relationship with you is removed. Forgive me, Lord. Once again I have done things my way.*

Would you pray that way?

God wants to intervene in your life. Although at this moment you may not see it, what is happening to you at this time is the best. It is true that we cannot understand how certain circumstances can benefit us or be good for us. How was Job to understand that everything that had happened to him was for his good, that after the time of struggle he would come to know God face to face? How was the ordinary Israelite who lived in fear and hidden in a cave to understand that this situation would end up being the best thing that could have happened to him?

Something similar happens to us. When we are immersed in difficult circumstances we cannot see clearly how much blessing there can be in them. But we need to trust God. And God wants to help us recognize our true spiritual condition.

We cannot grow without going through the moment of being honest with God and ourselves.

> *If we say we have no sin, we deceive ourselves, and the truth is not in us. If we confess our sins, he is faithful and just to forgive us our sins and to cleanse us from all unrighteousness.* (1 John 1: 8, 9)

Take God seriously. Listen to His voice when He remembers you what He already taught you . Agree with Him. If there is any area of your life where you have not been acting according to what God has taught you, acknowledge your situation and turn to Him.

God still wants to do a powerful work in your life. Bow down to God in humility and stand up to let Him renew and strengthen you.

Because there is still a long way to go.

A Different Conversation

Y ou may have had one of those days.

You are there, doing what you have to do. You haven't had a good week. What? Did I say a week? You haven't had a good year! And you can't get it out of your head. You turn ideas over and over again trying to make sense of the situation and more than anything trying to find a way out, although you have already thought about that something like a million times.

Then "someone" appears (you know, sometimes you don't even have the courage to look up to see who it is) who greets you happily or even tries to joke with you. But you are not for jokes.

Has something like this happened to you? Have you had one of those days?

How do you respond to that person? Some would try to stay calm and keep the good manners, being nice, even if it wouldn't be easy to be in the same sense of humor. Maybe he or she is having a good morning, but that is not your case.

What if there was more than casual communication in that conversation?

Surely you have already had some of those talks that leave a permanent trace on you. Most of us communicate with several dozen people a day. Do you remember everything you told them and everything they told you? No, of course, because the truth is that not all conversations have the same relevance. If you go to a doctor's appointment, you will want to keep what he tells you in as much detail as possible, but there are other conversations that you don't pay the same attention to. Did the supermarket cashier make a comment about the weather? Well, that's not the kind of thing that sticks in memory.

But there are different conversations. Actually, it usually isn't something you plan for. It is something that happens, it occurs. But when it happens, the result of that encounter, those shared words, those expressed emotions remain in the heart and can become the seed of future decisions, including the most important ones.

There are people who remember having conversations like this with their parents, their siblings, their best friends, but, with a stranger?

Did it ever happen to you? Have you ever had a deep and relevant conversation with a stranger that you may never hear from again? That is already less frequent, right?

I believe that, at least at first, that was what Gideon considered was happening to him on that occasion:

> *Now the angel of the Lord came and sat under the terebinth at Ophrah, which belonged to Joash the Abiezrite, while his son Gideon was beating out wheat in the winepress to hide it from the Midianites.*
>
> *And the angel of the Lord appeared to him and said to him,*
>
> *"The Lord is with you, O mighty man of valor."*
>
> *And Gideon said to him,*

"Please, my lord, if the Lord is with us, why then has all this happened to us? And where are all his wonderful deeds that our fathers recounted to us, saying, 'Did not the Lord bring us up from Egypt?' But now the Lord has forsaken us and given us into the hand of Midian."

And the Lord turned to him and said,

"Go in this might of yours and save Israel from the hand of Midian; do not I send you?"

And he said to him,

"Please, Lord, how can I save Israel? Behold, my clan is the weakest in Manasseh, and I am the least in my father's house."

And the Lord said to him,

"But I will be with you, and you shall strike the Midianites as one man." (Judges 6:11 - 16)

The occasion was that of the people of Israel when they were in a time of great difficulty. They were poor, worried, afraid, without seeing a way out of their situation.

The passage mentions that at that moment *the angel of the Lord came.*

I have to pause here to consider this with you. Angels are mentioned on different occasions throughout the Bible. There is even a definition that says: *"Are they not all ministering spirits sent out to serve for the sake of those who are to inherit salvation"* (Hebrews 1:14). Most of the biblical references to angels speak of *"angels"*, *"an angel"* of God, *"angels of the Lord"*. But it is different when **the angel of the Lord** is mentioned.

It is not just "one more". It is **the *angel*.**

Furthermore, it is interesting to observe that it is mentioned only in the Old Testament, not in the New. Why is it?

When we continue to delve into this story, it becomes clear that Gideon does not talk just with an envoy of God, but with God himself, and that even he himself ends up fearing for his own life, because of having had a talk with God himself in person.

This is why many of us interpret that the references to ***the angel of the Lord*** in the Old Testament are nothing less than mentions of the manifestation of God himself. And how do we explain the absence of such references in the New Testament? I think the answer to this question is quite simple: because in the New Testament Jesus is presented as the incarnation of God, as the presence of God himself, so that He no longer needs to present himself as *the angel*.

The people of Israel had felt overwhelmed by their situation of difficulty and defeat, and in their despair, in their anguish, they had cried out to God for help. In the beginning, in response, God had sent them a prophet, a messenger to make them reflect on their spiritual condition. The purpose was that the children of God would not leave their situation without recognizing their spiritual reality and what had led them to that time of tribulation.

Now, also in response to their cry, God had sent His angel to them.

I want you to pay close attention to this conversation, because I think it can make us reflect on the way God presents Himself to us, to this day.

Consider it from the point of view of Gideon, the son of Joash.

In the story we are provided with a geographic reference. Both the author and the first readers and listeners of this story could know the specific place where this had occurred. A place (Ophra) and a landmark (a terebinth, a tree) are mentioned in the text. What was there? A winepress.

The wineries were the sheds where the grapes were usually trodden for the production of wine. It was not the regular space to use as a warehouse for the wheat harvest. But in those difficult moments any place would be good, if it served to hide the grain from the eyes of the enemies. Those people worked hard to sow the land, to reap it, and then they could lose all the fruits of that effort if the enemies discovered them. So in addition to the effort, they had to live in fear that the profit resulting from their efforts would be taken away from them.

That was what Gideon was doing when *the angel of the Lord came*. He was threshing the wheat, separating the wheat grains from the branches, and storing in that hiding place. It was hard work, and under the circumstances he had to do it looking around from time to time to see if an enemy would come along, who might snatch their property.

We don't know what Gideon was thinking about when got involved in this conversation, but his answers give us the idea that he was not happy. That situation made him sad, uncomfortable, discouraged, broken.

His frame of mind was not the best, when this stranger (Gideon did not know at first that he was chatting with God) showed up and offered this unusual (and out of place, given the circumstances) greeting:

"The Lord is with you, O mighty man of valor."

Put yourself in Gideon's situation for a moment. You are focused on working, and at the same time you are worried, and your head does not stop spinning, weighing the situation in which you find yourself. Then someone shows up and greets you aloud with a "Good to see you, Champ!" How would you feel inside when you received the greeting?

To begin with, you may already feel uncomfortable enough with the unexpected and untimely greeting. You are fearing the arrival of an enemy and this subject appears to you, as if it came from nowhere! What a scare he could give you.

The passage does not reveal Gideon's private thoughts, but it does reveal his answer. Gideon had not only considered the unexpectedness of the greeting, but had also perceived the unusualness of its content. The visitor had said something that he had just been struggling with in his thoughts.

The Lord is with you ...!

That could have been considered nothing more than a casual greeting. To this day we use positive phrases when meeting. We say "Good morning" and "It's good to see you." Hebrew culture was no different in this regard. We know, for example, that they always used the term "Shalom" as a greeting, and its meaning is a wish for peace and prosperity.

But Gideon did not take it as casual.

When you read the beginning of this dialogue, what do you think Gideon's spirit is like? Come on, we have to admit it: Gideon didn't even try to be nice to the stranger.

> *"Please, my lord, if the Lord is with us, why then has all this happened to us? And where are all his wonderful deeds that our fathers recounted to us, saying, 'Did not the Lord bring us up from Egypt?' But now the Lord has forsaken us and given us into the hand of Midian."*

As we said, perhaps he had not even looked up from what he

was doing, and simply expressed what was already filling his mind. The visitor's greeting had just touched a delicate point.

Gideon had been told about God. He had heard of His promises and the covenant He had made with his ancestors. Perhaps he had even heard them talking that same day, or in previous days, mentioning the faithfulness of God and the greatness of the victories with which He had brought them to where they now lived.

But those stories did not fit the reality that he and his family faced at the time. It becomes evident that was what had been feeding his anxiety, and right now he has a precious opportunity to express it. The stranger's greeting had been enough to make him release what was in his heart.

We can compare this with one of "those days" when we respond to the classic morning greeting saying: "Good morning? Do you think these is a 'good morning'? For me, it's anything but good."

Now wait, before we get down to berating Gideon for his bad attitude or his lack of faith, what f we take a moment to identify ourselves within this story?

Has something like what happened to Gideon ever happen to you?

It may have not been a huge army endangering your life and that of your loved ones, or affecting the economy and social stability, holding you all in fear. What may have already happened to you is that after hearing about God, his power, his grace, his miracles, his mercy, you have compared all that with your own situation, with the difficult circumstances you're going through, only to conclude that you do not see the Almighty and merciful God in what you are living.

Do you know what I mean?

When life hits us, there are times when any of us, even knowing the Word of God, even having heard of the miracles and the love of God, may not make sense of what happens.

Most of us who believe in Jesus try to keep those thoughts away from us, or at least we don't make them known to others. What would they think of us if they knew that we harbor such "faithless" ideas like those?

Because, think about it, if we considered Gideon as if he was one of the Christians who congregate in one of our churches today, we would already be ready to rebuke him. How do you come to question God's presence or question His mighty miracles?

Because that's exactly what he did:

> *... if the Lord is with us, why then has all this happened to us?*

You see? This Old Testament hero is questioning God's presence with His people. As Gideon sees it, the resulting disaster and desolation did not correspond to a people in whose midst is God, the mighty, the Creator, the miracle worker.

This way of reasoning is not yours alone.

I have heard this complaint from quite a few people, especially those who do not attend church. When something bad happens, knowing that Christians preach a God of love, full of power, they throw comments such as: "If there was a loving God, these things would not happen." Such comments, far from being an attack on the church or on God, are neither more nor less than the expression of the pain that fills the hearts of these people. Yes, they are an expression of ignorance about the true God, and also a way of communicating their inability to understand what is happening. This was also the case with Gideon, who gave expression to his brokenness, brought by the reality that he had to experience.

Christians are generally more careful about what we say. We

avoid showing our confusion, and instead try to confess what we have learned, even if we do not always feel it. *WE KNOW* that all things help for good for those who love God, even though sometimes we don't understand why we have to face the problems that come our way.

Actually, there was an answer to Gideon's complaint. God could have spoken to him directly to teach him that He was with them (wasn't He right there, speaking to Gideon face to face?), and that even for those moments of struggle and discouragement there was a purpose. But he preferred a much more eloquent language than that of words, the language of the experience, so that His son would learn that principle.

Examine your heart for a moment. Is there a complaint inside you? Do not be ashamed. Anyway, God knows even the depths of your thoughts. Is there an area of your life where you don't understand God's purposes for what you are going through?

> *And where are all his wonderful deeds that our fathers recounted to us, saying, 'Did not the Lord bring us up from Egypt?' But now the Lord has forsaken us and given us into the hand of Midian.*

This is a point with which I feel very identified. At the beginning of my Christian life I was faced with these thoughts, and I assure you that they were something very clear and special to me. I had started to read the Bible, especially the New Testament, and there, for the first time I was reading about the wonderful miracles that Jesus had done. Those stories captivated me and deeply touched my heart, revealing to me that Jesus was much more than just a man, much more than any hero that our history has recorded. Those wonderful miracles proved that Jesus was the

Son of God, the only one capable of taking our place and granting us the benefit of salvation.

So I started reading the book of Acts. I was so excited! There I could almost see those heroes of the faith, the apostles and the brothers and sisters who were part of the early church in action, experiencing the fulfillment of Jesus' promises, His presence, and His work with every step they took. And they, too, experienced wonderful miracles! The paralytic in Jerusalem had been healed, the possessed woman in Philippi had been delivered, and even Peter's shadow had healed some!

It was then that those thoughts assailed me. They just coincided with times when I had been in contact with some Christians who spoke a lot about miracles and when I was going through difficult circumstances. You can imagine what thoughts came to me, right?

Yes, it was when I began to wonder why God did not perform those miracles in my own life, or why I did not see them in my congregation, since we were going through moments of difficulty in which God's miraculous intervention would have served us well. On several occasions I wondered why those Christians so lacking in many of the comforts that we enjoy today did have the opportunity to experience God in such a powerful and mighty way, since the same did not seem to be happening in my life. Was the same God who was with them, with me? Was the same Holy Spirit that had filled them, working in my life?

I thank God that He did not leave me in that ignorance. God, in his immense grace and faithfulness, began to show me His presence, His grace and also His miracles. Just as He did with Gideon.

Just as He will do with you if you commit your trust to Him.

Gideon had come to the conclusion that God was not there, that He had abandoned them. He may had intervened before, at some remote moment in history, but at that moment he saw no evidence of the presence and power of God in the situation they were experiencing.

That was a wrong conclusion. But God didn't correct him right away. Instead, He offered him to be part of the solution, and entrusted him with a mission.

And the Lord turned to him and said,

"Go in this might of yours and save Israel from the hand of Midian; do not I send you?"

Was God seeing the same person Gideon had seen in the mirror that morning when he got up?

That is what I ask myself sometimes when I read and receive God's comments about me.

How do you feel when you read passages like this?

Because you are precious in my eyes, and honored, and I love you, I give men in return for you, peoples in exchange for your life. Fear not, for I am with you … (Isaiah 43: 4, 5)

My first reaction is as if I looked around asking myself: "Are you talking to me?" Precious and worthy of honor? Worthy of being taken into account in the thoughts of the Creator of the universe?

The point is that many times we do not see what God is seeing when He looks at us. We see our failures, our weakness, our fears, our guilt, our unworthiness. God sees the person that He created, with all the potential to live at His level and face any circumstance with His presence and His power.

God revealed to Gideon that He already had what it took to break the cycle of defeat that he and his people were in.

It is interesting to note that God does not tell you that He is going to multiply your might. Do you realize that humans have fantasized about superheroes for years? True! We have considered that if we are to overcome our problems, superpowers are needed.

However, God sends Gideon to deliver Israel from oppression saying:

Go in this might of yours …

This man knew that his strength had its limitations. Until that moment, his strength had him secretly threshing wheat and full of fear that the enemies would discover him.

But God saw something else.

Could it be that God sees something else in you too?

Take it seriously. You may have had a narrow and diminished perspective on yourself up to this moment, and you need a dose of what God sees when he looks at you.

Like Gideon.

But he was not ready to seize God's perspective so quickly, and so he replied:

And he said to him,

"Please, Lord, how can I save Israel? Behold, my clan is the weakest in Manasseh, and I am the least in my father's house."

Look at this: despite the powerful words and the tremendous mission that God was entrusting him with, Gideon still felt insecure. It seems as if he had forgotten that God was backing him up with his authority (" *…do not I send you*"). Well, we can give him that at that time he was still not sure he was talking to God.

His words sound like he's saying, "Who? Me? Are you forgetting who you are talking to? I'm nobody!". This is how Gideon felt.

And you may feel that way sometimes, too.

There are many occasions when life presents us with challenges. These can appear in the form of problems or opportunities. It can happen that you are faced with a difficult problem to solve, such as when you go to the doctor and he has to tell you exactly what you do not want to hear. Then you are presented with the question of whether you will be able to cope with the disease and move on despite a negative diagnosis. Or it may be that you have the opportunity to study a university degree, and that at some point you wonder if you can finish it, because there are so many demands.

Thus, there are many moments in which we feel small, it seems to us that we are not up to the task, we consider that we are not capable of achieving it.

I am the least …

That's what Gideon said.

Was he?

You know? That may depend on your point of view.

For a young child who is shown for the first time the shape of an airplane crossing the sky, how big is that airplane? Well, "this small". Its size can be represented by the distance between the thumb and the pointing finger of a hand. But if you take the little one to the airport, there you can show him the true size of the aircraft. When he gets to have it right before him, his eyes will open very wide, as an expression of amazement. What was the difference? It's a matter of points of view. Seen from a great distance, the plane looks small, but when you get closer it will look big.

The same difference of views can occur in how we see ourselves and how God sees us.

God saw a mighty warrior where Gideon saw a frightened mouse. Time and experience proved that God was right.

God had an answer for the insignificant:

And the Lord said to him,

"But I will be with you, and you shall strike the Midianites as one man."

What Gideon was about to learn is what you and I also need to learn and experience. It can be formulated like this:

IT IS NOT THE SAME TO FACE CIRCUMSTANCES WITH GOD ON OUR SIDE THAN WITHOUT HIM.

When God addresses Gideon, He is not making a suggestion or speaking of a possibility. If He had been doing it, He would have just suggested what Gideon could do. But God doesn't do that. He speaks with authority. He affirms, without a doubt, what is going to happen. That's how strong the Word of God is.

In fact, even though he says *"You shall strike ... "*, God is affirming what **He** is going to do.

Those are the wonderful things God does in dealing with insignificants like us: He shares His victory. God was about to defeat His enemies, but announces to Gideon that he is going to defeat them.

God wants to share His victory with you too. I'm sure there are areas in your life where God wants to manifest His presence and power, and He wants to share that victory with you.

And, do you know why you will be able to celebrate that victory? So He said to Gideon:

I will be with you ...

God does not want to limit Himself to being "just God", disconnected from your life, away from your interests and the situations you face. When Jesus was born it was announced that He was the fulfillment of the prophecy that had anticipated that that child would be called "Immanuel" (Isaiah 7:14; Matthew 1:23). When Matthew wrote that part of the story, he took the trouble to write down what the meaning of that name was: it means "God with us."

For those of us who believe in Jesus, God is no longer "simply God", disconnected and absent, but is *God with us*, an active protagonist of everything we experience, a permanent companion and a faithful friend in all circumstances. The Word makes it clear to us that God is on our side (Romans 8:31) when we give Jesus our trust as our Lord and Savior.

That is why I know that if you received Jesus as Savior and Lord, He is with you, just as He was with Gideon.

And God has not changed. He has the same power, the same authority, and the same wisdom that He used to bring victory to this man from so long ago.

So think about it. God wants to relate with you personally. When He wanted to relate with Gideon, He came to sit under the same tree that gave him shade. God is going to appear where you are, in your city, among your people, and He is going to draw your attention precisely where you are. Think about it, because you don't want to walk past God and not pay your attention to Him. He already expressed His love for you when He gave his Son, that was sacrificed for you to have eternal life and you reconciled with Him.

Oddly enough, even a conversation with a stranger—or words

written by a perfect stranger, like those you are reading right now—can be used by God to reveal His presence and plans to you. God wants to have with you one of those conversations that leave permanent traces, and He wants to lead you through the difficulties that come your way in victory.

At the same time, God wants you to open your heart to Him and to honestly express what you feel. God led His people to victory using a man who had the courage to tell Him that he considered that He had not kept His promise to be with them, that He had abandoned them. If you don't feel Him, tell Him. If you don't see Him, don't keep it to yourself, express it in His presence. He prefers a sincere heart that says what it truly feels than lying lips that say the right words without feeling them.

And listen. God has something to tell you. He wants you to know how He sees you, and believe me, what He sees is different from what you see. Let Him be your mirror, let Him describe how you are. He knows more about you than you do, and He knows what is going to happen from now on. So listen to Him.

God still has a plan, and your participation in it is tremendously important. Those of us who believe in Jesus are rescuers: we draw lives from the rubble, we show the path of light to those who have totally lost notion and meaning. God wants to use you. Yes, you. Gideon, you and I are the insignificants that God can use to do things greater than our imaginations.

So prepare yourself. Let yourself be surprised by the powerful Owner of everything that exists, because He comes to propel you with the wings of His love.

With Much or Less Faith

Are you a person of faith?

Hard question! Don't you think? This could be one of those issues where you first evaluate who is asking the question before answering. Or else, since the answer does not come easily, you would ask in turn: "What do you mean by that?"

In this case I mean precisely that: Do you consider yourself a person of faith?

In a sense, you could interpret that we are being asked if you attend church. And if you attend your local church more or less regularly, you would answer that yes, that you are a person of faith, that you have your convictions more or less clear and that you profess them just as you have learned to do so.

But this same question could have another depth. I put myself in your shoes and try to respond, and almost automatically I answer to myself: "I would like to be a person of faith!"

Do you understand why?

Some of us think deeply before defining ourselves as people of faith. That has to do with the respect we have for this issue, and because we have become used to considering the testimonies of the lives of those who showed exemplary faith.

Have you read the stories in the Bible that tell us of the feats and victories experienced by those we consider "heroes of the faith"? How do you feel as you meditate on the account of historical moments like the one in which Moses raises his rod and the Red Sea parts, thus opening a path for God's people to pass? I don't know how you feel about them, but I am amazed when I consider these stories, and I am moved by the expression of the faith of those men and women who saw the impossible materialize, through the intervention of God.

And I want to have such a life.

And I want to have that kind of faith.

But then I reconsider my reality and the faith in my heart and I feel so small! I don't even dare to compare myself with Moses, with David, with Peter, with Paul. We generally consider them giants, people who reached a very special level of consecration, understanding and relationship with God, which allowed them to live such experiences.

The Bible, in a way, wants to offer us some comfort in this regard. That is why it says:

> *Elijah was a man with a nature like ours, and he prayed fervently that it might not rain, and for three years and six months it did not rain on the earth. Then he prayed again, and heaven gave rain, and the earth bore its fruit.* (James 5:17, 18)

My first reaction to these words might be, "Are you kidding me? Are you using Elijah as an example? Have you read the accounts regarding the life of Elijah since 1 Kings 17? Because of his prayers it stopped raining, and because of his prayers it rained again, it is true. But that was not the only thing that happened. He was miraculously fed, multiplied food, resurrected a widow's son, brought fire down from heaven, thus proving who the true God was! And are you going to tell me that *'he was a man with a nature like ours'*? Don't you realize how far my faith is from that of Elijah?"

Do you understand my conflict as you consider the lives of these heroes of faith and compare them with my own faith? Am I a person of faith? Well, I guess you can say that I am. I go to church, read the Bible, pray, believe in God, and praise Him. But men of faith were "those" …

Is that true?

Our meditation on this matter becomes even more delicate when we consider these words that we find in the letter to the Hebrews:

> *And without faith it is impossible to please him, for whoever would draw near to God must believe that he exists and that he rewards those who seek him.* (Hebrews 11: 6)

Pay attention to this teaching: if we are not people of faith *we cannot please God*.

The use of the term *"impossible"* is not very common in the Bible, and is almost always used to show the contrast between what men can (or cannot) do and what God can. Its use in this verse makes this statement very strong. If you don't have faith, you can't please God. And if you don't please God, you are lost.

If you think like I do, surely you want to please God. That means you want to be a person of faith.

Interesting how this verse expresses the reasons why it is important to have faith:

- You have to *believe that he exists*. That requires faith, because God is invisible.
- You have to believe that God *rewards those who seek him*. You need to believe that God accomplishes His promises.

Those two are very clear biblical truths. God exists and rewards those who seek Him. So, are you a person of faith?

Personally, I identify with Gideon's attitude when God presented Himself to him and told him that he was sending him to free his people from the oppression of their enemies. The man offered his excuses, his reasons why he did not consider this to be possible. And then this happened:

And he said to him,

"If now I have found favor in your eyes, then show me a sign that it is you who speak with me. Please do not depart from here until I come to you and bring out my present and set it before you."

And he said,

"I will stay till you return."

So Gideon went into his house and prepared a young goat and unleavened cakes from an ephah of flour. The meat he put in a basket, and the broth he put in a pot, and brought them to him under the terebinth and presented them.

And the angel of God said to him,

"Take the meat and the unleavened cakes, and put them on this rock, and pour the broth over them."

And he did so. Then the angel of the Lord reached out the tip of the staff that was in his hand and touched the meat and the unleavened cakes. And fire sprang up from the rock and consumed the meat and the unleavened cakes. And the angel of the Lord vanished from his sight.

Then Gideon perceived that he was the angel of the Lord. And Gideon said,

"Alas, O Lord God! For now I have seen the angel of the Lord face to face."

But the Lord said to him,

"Peace be to you. Do not fear; you shall not die."

Then Gideon built an altar there to the Lord and called it, The Lord Is Peace. To this day it still stands at Ophrah, which belongs to the Abiezrites. (Judges 6:17-24)

That had been a rather unusual and even uncomfortable situation. Not just Gideon and his family, but all of Israel was in dire trouble. The enemies were oppressing them, trampling their lands, consuming their resources, and were making it very difficult for them to survive. The people had cried out to God for help and He had sent them a prophet to help them recognize that they had done wrong, offending the Lord. Then *the angel of the Lord* had come to sit under an oak, just where Gideon was working, trying to hide the little grain harvested from his enemies. At the beginning Gideon did not know that it was God who was speaking to him, and he had expressed his doubts and even his frustration, because he considered that God had abandoned them, giving them into the hands of their enemies. But the answer that the angel gave him was that he himself would face the enemy army and free Israel from oppression. "Who? Me? "Gideon replied, although with other words, " I am nobody! ".

That man had had the audacity to question the reality of God's presence with His people. He felt and believed that God had abandoned them. This is what the situation they were in looked like to him. Furthermore, that he would free his people from oppression? This sounded ridiculous, out of place, impossible.

The angel of God had dropped a couple of sentences that suggested his true identity.

Do not I send you? (Judges 6:14)

I will be with you, and you shall strike … (Judges 6:16)

It is possible that these words were the ones that aroused doubt in Gideon's heart as to the identity of his interlocutor. Who else but God could have the authority to say such a thing?

A small shadow of doubt, a small thought in which he considered that perhaps it was God who was speaking to him, a small illusion that it might be true that he could go to face the enemies and defeat them began to raise in Gideon's heart.

Until then, would you consider Gideon a man of faith?

When you ponder his attitude and his responses, what seems to stand out is the fact that all he had done was doubt, question, confess his defeat.

But what I would like you to notice in this story is the way in which God himself is in charge of awakening and feeding faith in the heart of that man. I want you to notice it, because this is how God works in your life too.

God wants your heart to be filled with faith.

God wants to do his work—powerful, wonderful, divine— through you, just as he did through Gideon.

So the other question that arises here is: how much faith does it take to participate in the miracles that God does? How much faith does it take to be one of those people who experience God doing the impossible?

Many of us have the concept that the men and women of God who experienced great miracles in their lives through God's intervention were very self-assured, balanced people who never experienced a moment of doubt. But consider Gideon. He is also in the gallery of the heroes of faith in Hebrews 11:

> *And what more shall I say? For time would fail me to tell of Gideon, Barak, Samson, Jephthah, of David and Samuel and the prophets— who through faith conquered kingdoms, enforced justice, obtained promises, stopped the mouths of lions, quenched the power of fire, escaped the edge of the sword, were made strong out of weakness, became mighty in war, put foreign armies to flight.* (Hebrews 11:32 - 34)

There you have him, among the great ones, mentioned before David, Samuel and the prophets. Among those who *obtained promises.*

You know? Your name would have to appear there too, because you want to please God, and therefore you are a person of faith. Yes, your name.

So how much faith does it take to please God?

The story of the man whose son was possessed by an evil spirit comes to mind. He had brought him to Jesus, but He was just on the mountain where Peter, James and John saw the blaze of His glory. So the disciples there had tried to heal the boy, without success. When the Master arrived they presented the case to Him, and He regretted their lack of faith.

As you will notice, this "enough faith" business is something that has troubled people for a long time.

This is what happened then:

And Jesus asked his father,

"How long has this been happening to him?"

And he said,

"From childhood. And it has often cast him into fire and into water, to destroy him. But if you can do anything, have compassion on us and help us."

And Jesus said to him,

"'If you can'! All things are possible for one who believes."

Immediately the father of the child cried out and said,

"I believe; help my unbelief!" (Mark 9:21 - 24)

That father wanted the best for his son, he wanted him to be free and healthy. It is like someone who comes to the doctor's room bringing their sick loved one. You too would say to the doctor something like: "Doctor, if you can do something to make him better, please do it!"

Jesus did not let go of the doubt that the man had expressed. He used the same phrase as him ("if you can") to declare the importance of faith:

If you can! All things are possible for one who believes.

This is a shocking statement. Do you realize what it implies? This is one of those words that applies to everyone who meets the conditions. In this case, the condition is to *believe* . And what happens to the one who believes? For that person *all things are possible.*

It is there that you and I stumble many times. We do not consider ourselves worthy of the definition, it seems to us that we will never meet the requirement, on the condition of *believing* . It occurs to us that "those people" for whom "all things are possible" are not us. They are "those" heroes of faith that populate the pages of the Bible and history, being only a few and appearing from time to time.

But if that were so, you and I could not please God, because it is impossible to do it without faith. I believe that the boy's father left us a very great lesson, worthy of serious consideration and imitation.

Immediately the father of the child cried out and said,

"I believe; help my unbelief!"

This man was overflowing with love for his son. He really wanted to see him free, developing healthily. He wanted to see him play happily with the other children, without the limitations that had held him down until that day.

Was faith a condition for his son to be healthy? Was believing that Jesus could do it the requirement for the miracle to occur? Then *"Yes"* was his reply, *"I believe."* Perhaps internally he knew that what he was really expressing was "I want to believe!" That is why he added his desperate request for help: *"...help my unbelief!"*.

If instead of having Jesus materially in front of him this man had been praying, would you consider this to be what we sometimes call "a powerful prayer"? Doesn't seem like it, right?

But I think this last sentence would have to be our prayer.

Because you know what? That was the prayer that Jesus answered with the healing and deliverance of that man's son! That prayer was powerful, in the sense that it generated the miracle of healing on the boy's life!

Did that man have what we call "a lot of faith"? According to our definition, it appears that he did not . However, his request was heard, his cry was answered, and the miracle occurred.

Let's not forget about the disciples. They had tried to do it before, and couldn't. Now they had seen how Jesus had taken authority over the situation and released the boy. Matthew tells us that later, when they were alone with the Master, this dialogue took place:

> *Then the disciples came to Jesus privately and said,*
>
> *"Why could we not cast it out?"*
>
> *He said to them,*
>
> *"Because of your little faith. For truly, I say to you, if you have faith like a grain of mustard seed, you will say to this mountain, 'Move from here to there,' and it will move, and nothing will be impossible for you."*
> (Matthew 17:19-21)

So they had not been able to produce the miracle because they had little faith. That would be consistent with our concept in this regard. They were not like Moses, like Elijah … But Jesus added that of the size of faith.

The faith that moves the hand of God, the faith that produces mighty miracles, is the size of a mustard seed. The disciples knew what the Master was talking about. The mustard seed is between one and two millimeters in diameter. At least twenty to twenty-five mustard seeds will fit on the nail of your thumb. That's how great is the faith necessary, no longer to free a possessed boy, but to move a mountain from place.

What was Jesus talking about? That it is not a matter of great faith, but of faith. It is not that some people lives are at a higher level than other mortals. That is what we sometimes think of people of faith. It's not like that. Elijah was truly an ordinary man, with doubts and weaknesses as well, and he even became depressed. Same with the rest. The same is true for the father who cried out for his son, asking for help for his unbelieving heart.

The same as Gideon.

Gideon doubted that he was talking to God. He doubted that it was God who was giving him the task—the immense task—of freeing his people from oppression. Gideon also asked for help to overcome the unbelief in his heart.

> *"If now I have found favor in your eyes, then show me a sign that it is you who speak with me. Please do not depart from here until I come to you and bring out my present and set it before you."*

Gideon was also a *man of little faith.* Do you realize what he's asking from God?

> *… show me a sign that it is you who speak with me.*

I identify myself so much with these words! Yes, I too many times have needed—and many times I need—for God to confirm that it is He who speaks to me.

And you? Do you also need God to confirm His Word, for God to strengthen your faith?

That's how fragile we are. People of faith are not superheroes who stand firm and steady no matter what the situation is presented to them. They are human beings who sometimes break down, who doubt, for whom fear and confusion are not strange.

Gideon was like that too. And what was God's attitude toward his doubts? That man was saying to God: "I'm not sure it's you who is speaking to me; confirm it, please." What did God do? Did He reproached him for his lack of faith? Did He go looking for someone else who had more faith?

No. God got ready to confirm His presence, His power and His personal interest in intervening in that difficult situation they faced.

God fed Gideon's faith.

He also wants to feed yours.

Gideon went, prepared a meal dedicated to his visitor, produced the best he had. Observe that when he wanted a confirmation of the presence of God with him, what he did was to present an offering.

His attitude was not the same as that of those who doubted that God was present and at work.

So they said to him,

"Then what sign do you do, that we may see and believe you? What work do you perform? (John 6:30)

Do you know who these were, the ones who asked these question? They were the same ones who had just been fed with the five loaves and two fish that Jesus multiplied. They had listened to the Son of God, had seen the miracle and benefited from it, and still asked for "a sign" by which Jesus would show them who He was.

This was not faith. It was abuse. Those people did not see that Jesus was the Son of God. They just wanted to witness the spectacular nature of another miracle. The Master did not answer them as expected and they ended up turning away from Him.

So there are different ways of expressing the need to believe. You can do it out of personal ambition or because you are truly seeking to relate to God and live in His will.

Gideon's story is that of a person whose faith grows, fueled by his relationship with God.

This is how your story has to be too.

You may also give offerings to God, as Gideon did. For you too, God can confirm that He receives and appreciates your offering.

> *Then Gideon perceived that he was the angel of the Lord. And Gideon said,*
>
> *"Alas, O Lord God! For now I have seen the angel of the Lord face to face."*
>
> *But the Lord said to him,*
>
> *"Peace be to you. Do not fear; you shall not die."*

Gideon would not easily emerge from his amazement. He had gone to prepare the offering and had brought it, he had done what the angel had told him and had put his offering in the place He had indicated. But then he had seen how that offering had been consumed by fire, and that was something he had not expected.

Did you notice what his first reaction was when that happened? He got scared! He experienced how great it is to talk to God face to face, to relate with his Creator, with Him who made the promises and keeps them. God knew that he thought he would die for having dealt directly with God, and so He consoled him by affirming that he would not die.

Today's disciples of Jesus relate to the same God that Gideon related to. It's still tremendous, but sometimes in the habit of doing it, we fail to appreciate the importance of those powerful and sublime moments when we connect with our mighty Savior.

When you pray in the name of Jesus, you are speaking to Him who can do everything, you are addressing the One who has all authority and all dominion. And the best thing is that He listens to you, and responds to you.

Some of us might have regarded Gideon as a basket case when it comes to faith. This man expressed very important doubts, born of his analysis of the circumstances that he and his people were facing. Can someone so incredulous receive anything from God? The story of Gideon shows us how God worked in his life, developing his faith when it seemed that all he had was doubts and unbelief.

How did He do it? How did God awaken and develop faith in the heart of this man beaten by life and difficulties? The Gideon we see at the end of the story—going into a humanly impossible battle and returning with a shocking victory—looks like "another person", compared to his initial attitude!

God visited him and confirmed His presence.

God did not rebuke him when he hesitated, but offered him confirmations.

God spoke to him clearly, stopping to confirm and clarify every step he had to take.

This is what God wants to do in your life too. Do you think that God doesn't know your heart's content? Of course He knows everything about you! He knows when you doubt and knows when you believe.

It may be that God is speaking to your heart right now. You do well if you ask Him: "Is it you, Lord?" Gideon did, and God confirmed His presence.

It can also happen to you that what God proposes, the mission

He wants to take you to, seems impossible. That was what Gideon thought too, and God leaded him through the process of understanding and trust, until he was willing to do anything to live in God's will. Is it hard for you to believe that God will do what you feel He is saying to you? You can tell him.

God wants to feed your faith.

God wants to use you.

God wants to answer your questions.

God wants to lead you to live what seems impossible to you.

God is working in your life. Get closer to Him and trust.

Facing Personal Obstacles

I have some questions for you:

- Make a brief reflection on your life, on how you are living at this time. Do you consider that something needs to be changed? Is there something that needs to be left behind or improved?
- What have you received from your family, your ancestors, your references? Do you think you have to respect their values and ideas or do you think you would have to change some of them?
- Is there something in your life that you accept because it is normal for others, even if it is not for you? Is it time to stand firm and put it aside, or is it better to keep going with the flow?

I am asking you these questions because I believe that this is what each of us needs to analyze personally, not just once but periodically.

We are all the product of our environment, our education, our time, our family, who have been our references. The experiences you have had throughout your life have determined who you are right now, including the way you make decisions, the way you relate to others, your habits and much more. At the same time, none of us is perfect; in other words, all of us can find aspects of our lives in which we have to change.

We all get those special moments when we come to the conclusion that we need a change. When we find that certain patterns of behavior or inherited values are not working well, it is time to change.

But it is not easy. Many times we prefer to stay with the known rather than change, "because we don't know what will happen to us if we change." Yes, we all, in a certain way, resist change, especially when it involves acting, behaving or thinking differently from those who live around us or the people with whom we usually interact. What are they going to say?

Some time ago I was diagnosed with diabetes. As many people know, this represents a major lifestyle change, particularly in terms of eating and exercising habits. I could have alleged that I really liked having a soda every now and then or that I had certain desserts that I considered my favorites, and that I definitely didn't want to permanently say goodbye to any of that. But I had to be flexible, apply common sense, and make a decision for what I knew was better stewardship of the body that God has given me. So goodbye soft drinks and desserts, some of which accompanied me for a good part of my journey in life. In the same way, sometimes we have to abandon habits, concepts, practices, attitudes and other characteristics of our existence when we are faced with the fact that they are harmful to ourselves and those around us. It turned out that sugar was a poison to me, and also other aspects of my life that I had to change.

This especially applies to those of us who have believed in Jesus and have decided to be His disciples. From that first moment when we have encountered the reality that Jesus is the only Way to eternal life and a restored relationship with God, the Holy Spirit of God helps us to recognize areas of our lives where we were polluting ourselves, with which we were offending God and that we needed (and many times still need) to change.

And sometimes, that is precisely what separates us from the work that God, in His immense love and according to His eternal plan, wants to develop in us.

> *And you were dead in the trespasses and sins in which you once walked, following the course of this world, following the prince of the power of the air, the spirit that is now at work in the sons of disobedience— among whom we all once lived in the passions of our flesh, carrying out the desires of the body and the mind, and were by nature children of wrath, like the rest of mankind. But God, being rich in mercy, because of the great love with which he loved us, even when we were dead in our trespasses, made us alive together with Christ—by grace you have been saved— and raised us up with him and seated us with him in the heavenly places in Christ Jesus, so that in the coming ages he might show the immeasurable riches of his grace in kindness toward us in Christ Jesus. For by grace you have been saved through faith. And this is not your own doing; it is the gift of God, not a result of works, so that no one may boast. For we are his workmanship, created in Christ Jesus for good works, which God prepared beforehand, that we should walk in them.* (**Ephesians 2: 1–10**)

It happens that believing in Jesus—we will never tire of saying it—is much more than an ideological or religious change. It is truly a personal revolution, and a true transformation from death to life. Many have fantasized about zombies, or the walking dead, when the real dead who think, talk and walk are all those who walk this life without Christ, that is, us, at some point in our existence, before the light of the gospel illuminated our hearts.

It is not that at some point in our life we were right with God before making our voluntary commitment of faith to Jesus. The life of any person disconnected from the vital relationship with God that can only be achieved by faith in Jesus, is defined as death in the Bible.

The person who does not listen to the voice of God and obeys Him, who does he or she obeys? It may seem that the person is independent, acting according to the dictates of his/her own heart, freely, but this passage teaches that he/she obeys the devil, and what is even worse, that he/she is the *object of God's anger*. It is by no means a position we want to be in, but we cannot get out of it until we accept God's guidance and decide to allow ourselves to be led by Him.

If you are recognizing at this moment that this is your situation, please make up your mind right now for Jesus, invoke His name, give Him your whole being and accept Him to be your Savior and the Lord of your life.

Some, perhaps, could argue: "I already experienced the transformation of my life when I believed in Jesus, some time ago ." That is where we fall into another error, because the reality is that while we are in the flesh we are going to find areas of our life that have to be subjected to the will of God, aspects of our existence that have to change.

Something like this is what happened to Gideon, just when God was calling him to live the immense adventure of participating in His work and witnessing His miracles. God wanted to integrate him into the development of His plan, to have him personally participate in what He was doing in response to the prayers of

His people, but first he needed to face the spiritual obstacles that perhaps Gideon had not considered until that moment.

That night the Lord said to him,

"Take your father's bull, and the second bull seven years old, and pull down the altar of Baal that your father has, and cut down the Asherah that is beside it and build an altar to the Lord your God on the top of the stronghold here, with stones laid in due order. Then take the second bull and offer it as a burnt offering with the wood of the Asherah that you shall cut down."

So Gideon took ten men of his servants and did as the Lord had told him. But because he was too afraid of his family and the men of the town to do it by day, he did it by night.

When the men of the town rose early in the morning, behold, the altar of Baal was broken down, and the Asherah beside it was cut down, and the second bull was offered on the altar that had been built. And they said to one another,

"Who has done this thing?"

And after they had searched and inquired, they said,

"Gideon the son of Joash has done this thing."

Then the men of the town said to Joash,

"Bring out your son, that he may die, for he has broken down the altar of Baal and cut down the Asherah beside it."

But Joash said to all who stood against him,

"Will you contend for Baal? Or will you save him? Whoever contends for him shall be put to death by morning. If he is a god, let him contend for himself, because his altar has been broken down."

Therefore on that day Gideon was called Jerubbaal, that is to say, "Let Baal contend against him," because he broke down his altar. (Judges 6:25 - 32)

Gideon was in a difficult and special situation. He was living, together with his family, moments of great difficulty, having to face the presence of military enemies that affected the life of the entire community in every way. Everything was wrong: the economy, relationships, activities that had previously been normal, everything was affected by fear, injustice and uncertainty.

So, while deep inside he would wonder where he could flee, while looking around fearing that the enemies would discover him hiding the product of the harvest, he received an amazing and different visit . It had taken him a bit to understand it at first, but he had managed to understand that God's angel had visited him. He had never expected something like that. Not in his wildest dreams would he have considered himself worthy of being remembered by God, much less being called by Him so that all his people could be freed from their enemies. But that had happened, no matter how hard it was for him to believe it.

Had Gideon ever wondered, before this event, what it would

be like or what it would feel like to have an encounter with God? And you? Have you met God? How has it been for you?

There are people who believe that God appears in a person's life and from that moment on everything goes well and is easy. If that's what you think too, I imagine this Gideon experience may make you reconsider your position.

Sometimes, before getting better, things can get even more difficult or uncomfortable. That is what happened to Gideon.

God himself was with him and his community, and had revealed Himself to him personally, confirming His presence without leaving any doubts about it. Now everything was just going to be okay, right?

No so fast! Before any victory, before more miracles, God demanded delicate, radical and very unpopular decisions.

The angel of God disappeared from Gideon's sight, but God spoke to him again that night. How did he speak to him? As so often in the Bible, we are not told the "how." It could have been a voice in his heart, a dream, a thought, or something else. What we do know is that God spoke to him, and that Gideon knew that He had done it, and he understood clearly what He said.

> *That night the Lord said to him,*

> *"Take your father's bull, and the second bull seven years old, and pull down the altar of Baal that your father has, and cut down the Asherah that is beside it and build an altar to the Lord your God on the top of the stronghold here, with stones laid in due order. Then take the second bull and offer it as a burnt offering with the wood of the Asherah that you shall cut down."*

Consider the way God speaks to Gideon in this passage. This is how He can and wants to talk to you. What does this passage tell you about God and the relationship he establishes with his children?

Do you realize how detailed and specific God is when ordering the steps of those who serve him? Consider the different ways he could have said it:

- "I have taught my people that idolatry is not a good thing. Teach your people that everything that is happening to them has to do with their bad habit of worshiping idols".
- "Gideon, have you ever bowed down to a pagan idol? Repent of that and all your sins".
- "Make a beautiful altar for God, and invite everyone who wants to believe to have a moment of adoration and gratitude in His presence."

You just read it, God didn't say anything like that . Read it again and consider the things he talked about.

- He mentioned his father's herd, that is, he knew perfectly well what the family business was.
- He specifically referred to one of the bulls, specifically the second. God did not limit Himself to knowing what the family's business was, but He also knew the details, what was discussed in the privacy of the family.
- Did you notice that God still refers to the age of the bull? He did not want Gideon to have reason to be wrong. This was a special bull, probably the best of the herd, and God had deemed it worthy of being a sacrifice to Him.
- God decided to choose with which wood the fire would be lit to burn the sacrificed bull as a holocaust. In the

selection of the firewood was contained the message that God wanted to transmit against idolatry. But He is still specific, very specific: he describes the altar dedicated to Baal and the post with the image of the goddess Ashera as one who has walked in front of the place. Gideon knew the place well, and he knew that the references were accurate.

• God not only knew the place . It all became absolutely personal for Gideon when he said *"the altar of Baal that your father has. "* It was not just any altar, "an altar", but God knew the origins, the reasons, the people involved. If Gideon himself had ever presented an offering to the pagan god, or if he had even bowed slightly in that place, God knew.

Do you understand what this reveals about God? Yes, you can say it: that God knows everything about people's lives, down to the smallest details. Do you realize that just as God knew the second bull of that herd and had seen the post dedicated to the goddess, in the same way He knows all the details of your existence?

King David, many years later, would discover this poignant reality.

> ¹   *O Lord, you have searched me and known me!*
> ²   *You know when I sit down and when I rise up;*
>   *you discern my thoughts from afar.*
> ³   *You search out my path and my lying down and*
>   *are acquainted with all my ways.*
> ⁴   *Even before a word is on my tongue, behold, O*
>   *Lord, you know it altogether.*
> ⁵   *You hem me in, behind and before, and lay your*
>   *hand upon me.*

⁶ *Such knowledge is too wonderful for me; it is high; I cannot attain it.*

⁷ *Where shall I go from your Spirit? Or where shall I flee from your presence?*

⁸ *If I ascend to heaven, you are there! If I make my bed in Sheol, you are there!*

⁹ *If I take the wings of the morning and dwell in the uttermost parts of the sea,*

¹⁰ *even there your hand shall lead me, and your right hand shall hold me.*

¹¹ *If I say, "Surely the darkness shall cover me, and the light about me be night,"*

¹² *even the darkness is not dark to you; the night is bright as the day, for darkness is as light with you.*

¹³ *For you formed my inward parts; you knitted me together in my mother's womb.*

¹⁴ *I praise you, for I am fearfully and wonderfully made. Wonderful are your works; my soul knows it very well.*

¹⁵ *My frame was not hidden from you, when I was being made in secret, intricately woven in the depths of the earth.*

¹⁶ *Your eyes saw my unformed substance; in your book were written, every one of them, the days that were formed for me, when as yet there was none of them.*

¹⁷ *How precious to me are your thoughts, O God! How vast is the sum of them!*

¹⁸ *If I would count them, they are more than the sand. I awake, and I am still with you.* (Psalms 139.1–18)

What a wonderful way to put it! No one can escape the gaze of God. He knows all the details of our existence. He knows our words even before they leave our mouth, He knows and knew the most intimate details of our body because He himself interwoven it. And the discovery of God's watchful eye to every corner of our existence is a wonderful thing!

> *And no creature is hidden from his sight, but all are naked and exposed to the eyes of him to whom we must give account.* (Heb. 4.13)

No, none, and that includes you. You were also created, and you are in the sight of God.

Doesn't your skin crawl as you consider this profound reality?

But wait! What do we immediately think of when reacting to the truth that God knows everything about us? Yes, we are almost immediately faced with the reality that there are aspects of our history that we are not exactly proud of. We have done, said, and thought things that have offended God, and we know it. We have disrespected Him in different ways, and that is called sin.

Yes, God had walked through the town where Gideon lived, and had been looking at the day when his father, his own father, had dedicated the altar to Baal. God had walked through that square where the Ashera post was located, and whoever knew the second bull in the herd, surely also knew each and every person in the community.

Just as He knows you, with your history, your facts, your mistakes and successes, your problems and your emotions.

But God did not stop at knowledge. Something had to be done about it, and God had been very specific about what to do. There was no room for wrong interpretations or inappropriate procedures.

This is perhaps the most direct teaching in this passage: ***Many times, in the process for God to answer our prayer to defeat our worst enemies He will ask us to abandon the corrupt ways that got us there in the first place.***

It is possible that we could have come up with a shortcut, an easier way to do it. We might think that, given that God is good and loves us, sometimes He could avoid the uncomfortable issues, to go specifically just to bless us and help us. But He doesn't do it like that, and do you know why? Because He knows that the most important thing in our lives is our relationship with Him. We were created to honor Him, and when we don't, when we put aside the fear of God to do things our way, we are the first to hurt ourselves.

That is why God is never going to overlook the issue of idolatry.

That was what happened on that occasion. God had heard the cry of his people, and He wanted to free them from their oppressors. But He couldn't do it as long as they continued to give a place of importance to something that was not Himself.

As you go through the pages of the Bible you will discover that this is a recurring theme. It appears among the commandments, it is reiterated over and over again in the Law, it is repeated throughout biblical history and even Jesus mentions that the most important commandment of all is that we love God above everything else.

Does this matter of idolatry have something to do with you? Is it just a matter of carved images? No, it's about God having to have your full attention, without someone or something distracting you from it.

Gideon had to face a very uncomfortable situation. God had given him very precise instructions about the first thing he had to do to serve Him, and that involved exposing himself publicly, speaking out against something that seemed good and normal to everyone.

I think we can relate to this. There are many things in the

society we live in that are normal, fun, and positive for most, but that alienate people from God. Do you find the parallel between what God asked Gideon to do and what He can ask of you and me? Today it is uncomfortable to talk about abortion, homosexuality, pornography, and many other sensitive topics. It is possible that God wants us to take the second bull and sacrifice it on the wood of those images.

> *So Gideon took ten men of his servants and did as the Lord had told him.*

I believe that God wants to find this kind of commitment and loyalty in us. Will it be easy? It will not always be, as it must not have been for Gideon. He avoided public exposure that would have meant to proceed with the destruction of the altar and the post in the full light of day, but he knew that anyway there would be reactions, and there were. Yes, Gideon must have been everyone's comment the following day.

> *When the men of the town rose early in the morning, behold, the altar of Baal was broken down, and the Asherah beside it was cut down, and the second bull was offered on the altar that had been built. And they said to one another,*

> *"Who has done this thing?"*

> *And after they had searched and inquired, they said,*

> *"Gideon the son of Joash has done this thing."*

> *Then the men of the town said to Joash,*

"Bring out your son, that he may die, for he has broken down the altar of Baal and cut down the Asherah beside it."

But Joash said to all who stood against him,

"Will you contend for Baal? Or will you save him? Whoever contends for him shall be put to death by morning. If he is a god, let him contend for himself, because his altar has been broken down."

Yes, there were those who wanted to "do something about it." There were those who considered that the son of Joash had gone too far. How was he going to go against the opinion of others? And yes, they wanted to take his life for that.

All of this makes me feel that most of the time we are faced with less resistance than he did.

God wants to deal with those delicate and uncomfortable issues in our life. He will not bless us or lead us to victory in His name while the idols are still standing. So we need to face the discomfort of standing before the light of God.

This is the message we have heard from him and proclaim to you, that God is light, and in him is no darkness at all. If we say we have fellowship with him while we walk in darkness, we lie and do not practice the truth. But if we walk in the light, as he is in the light, we have fellowship with one another, and the blood of Jesus his Son cleanses us from all sin. If we say we have no sin, we deceive ourselves, and the truth is not in us. If we confess our sins, he is faithful and just to forgive us our sins and to cleanse us from all unrighteousness. (1 John 1.5–9)

Let the Holy Spirit of God analyze your life and lead you to what needs to be done so that God can take His rightful place in your life. God is inviting you to participate in His work, to be a part of His victories and to be a witness of His miracles, but He has to count on your complete loyalty and a commitment to serve Him despite the opposition of those who do not serve Him, even if they are part of your family.

I invite you to stop reading and take some time to ask God to show you if any of this affects you personally. God knows how to do this in the most specific way possible, as He did with Gideon.

There is a great victory ahead. Trust God and take the steps of faith that He shows you. God is going to do something great, and He wants you to be a part of it.

Searching For God's Will

What are you doing with your life?

I know that formulated like this it sounds like a complicated question. I mean, it's not something you can answer right away. You need to think about it. But the fact that it makes you think is not bad. This is a complex question, and at the same time necessary for good personal development.

So try again. What are you doing with your life? What are you spending your time on? What are you going to dedicate the remaining years of your life to? Please, think about it.

And one step further in your personal meditation: Who do you serve? Who do you do what you do for? Who do you obey?

When you make decisions, whose will are you doing?

You can answer me that you are a free person, and I will understand. You make your own decisions, so it is obvious that you are doing your own thing.

Are you absolutely sure?

Do you know why I ask you? Because it can happen that without you noticing, you may end up falling under the subtleties of the world we live in, serving who you would not have wanted.

Think about it for a moment. Hasn't it ever happened to you that you come home after spending some time in a store, the supermarket or the mall and when you arrive you recognize that you bought something that you didn't really need? "Well, it was very cheap," you can argue. But was it really necessary? It looked good, it was accessible, it didn't seem like it was going to represent a very detrimental financial burden on your budget, but it wasn't essential. Whose will did you do in that case?

We all want to be free, have our own criteria and do things our way. The problem is that we often end up, in very subtle ways, serving masters we have not chosen or would never have wanted to serve.

Surely that is not what you want for yourself.

Nor is it what God wants for you. Rather, through Jesus and His sacrifice on the cross, God provided the means for us to consciously and deliberately choose whom to serve.

That is the reason why it is important that you question yourself again:

Why do you do what you do?

What is the basis on which you support your decisions?

Are you making the right decisions?

And for you who have already accepted that Jesus is the Savior and Lord of your life, to what extent do you care to DO THE WILL OF GOD?

Big question: Are you living according to God's will?

1. **Who or What Runs Your Life?**

Let me put this simply and directly: if you are not living in the will of God, you are living according to the will of someone else. You can argue that you do what you want, that you make your own decisions, that you do not accept pressure or manipulation from anyone. Yes, that may seem, but it is not the whole truth.

> *And you were dead in the trespasses and sins in which you once walked, following the course of this world, following the prince of the power of the air, the spirit that is now at work in the sons of disobedience— among whom we all once lived in the passions of our flesh, carrying out the desires of the body and the mind, and were by nature children of wrath, like the rest of mankind. But God, being rich in mercy, because of the great love with which he loved us, …* (Ephesians 2:1 - 4)

I think this is pretty clear. If Christ Jesus is not directing your life, if he is not your Lord, then you are living under the influence of other lords. Do you realize that it says here that those who do not live under the lordship of Christ live

- *following the course of this world,*
- *following the prince of the power of the air, the spirit that is now at work in the sons of disobedience,*
- *in the passions of the flesh,*
- *carrying out the desires of the body and the mind?*

Yes, it refers to making their own decisions (they follow their own will and their purposes), but they do so under the influence of *the spirit that is now at work in the sons of disobedience.* That sounds pretty bad, doesn't it?

That is, if you are not living in the will of God through faith in Jesus, do you really want to live *following the course of this world?* Do you realize that living like this has consequences for the present and also for the future?

So, wake up! It is vitally important that you make sure you are living what you have to live, according to the will of God. You need to confirm that it is God you are serving, rather than attempting to serve yourself, a member of your family, your boss and his money, and ultimately some spiritual power contrary to God's purposes.

The Word of God reveals to us what happened to Israel in the Promised Land after the conquest.

> *In those days there was no king in Israel. Everyone did what was right in his own eyes.* (Judges 21:25)

It seems too much like what happens in our present, don't you think? *Each one does what is right in his own eyes.*

If you stop to think carefully about your own life, you will have to recognize that we often live like this. Isn't that what everyone does? Because, what is wrong with *each one doing what is right in his own eyes*?

What's wrong is that *what seems right to us is* not always the best. And we are easy prey to the spiritual influence of the powers of this world, whose ideas are not exactly for our good.

The Word of God shows time and again its effectiveness in describing the people and the world in which we live. Notice how he describes the people of *the last days* .

> *But understand this, that in the last days there will come times of difficulty. For people will be lovers of self, lovers of money, proud, arrogant, abusive, disobedient to their parents, ungrateful, unholy, heartless, unappeasable, slanderous, without self-control, brutal, not loving good, treacherous, reckless, swollen with conceit, lovers of pleasure rather than lovers of God,*

having the appearance of godliness, but denying its power. Avoid such people. (2 Timothy 3:1 - 5)

The detail at the end is not of minor importance. Living without Christ and having all these kinds of attitudes and behaviors contrary to the will of God, a person could *have the appearance of godliness,* that is, see themselves as spiritual.

Please do not fall into this error.

The life that Jesus proposes us to live, being saved by His sacrifice on the cross, is very different.

> *Then Jesus told his disciples,*
>
> *"If anyone would come after me, let him deny himself and take up his cross and follow me. For whoever would save his life will lose it, but whoever loses his life for my sake will find it. For what will it profit a man if he gains the whole world and forfeits his soul? Or what shall a man give in return for his soul?* (Matthew 16:24 - 26)

It may look like a play on words, but it is much more than that.

Jesus makes clear how to establish a relationship with Him and with our heavenly Father through Him. Jesus is not looking for sympathizers, nor does he try to add up the number of people who like Him. Jesus saves the disciples, not the fans.

I believe that in these words of the Master it is very clear that a person cannot live life *in his own way* and be a disciple of Jesus at the same time. To be a disciple of Jesus you have to …

- … *deny yourself,*
- *take up your cross and*
- *follow Him.*

But do not miss the clarification that Jesus makes. A person may intend to *save his life*, and that person *will lose it* . The person who *finds his life* (the one who receives eternal life, real life) is the one who *loses his life* .

What is the Master referring to? He is informing us that any attempt to live life "our way", according to our own desires (and that implies living under the influence of the spiritual powers of this world) leads to damnation!

Do you understand why it is important to make sure you are living *according to the will of God*?

So, excuse the insistence but, whose will are you doing in your life?

2. **God Wants to Lead Your Life and That You Live According to His Will.**

No words are able to emphasize enough the freedom we come to experience when we truly live in the will of God.

When you live on your own, under the influence of the powers of this world, you may have the concept that living in the will of God is not pleasant, that it is just difficult, or that it is a life of limitations and deprivation. That is not true.

Nor is it true that God wants to hide His will, or that He has made it so difficult for believers to live according to His plans that only a few "very enlightened" are capable of living like this.

God wants **you to** live according to His will.

Do you remember the strong teaching Jesus pronounced about the timing of his second coming?

> *"Not everyone who says to me, 'Lord, Lord,' will enter the kingdom of heaven, but the one who does the will of my Father who is in heaven. On that day many will say to me, 'Lord, Lord, did we not prophesy in*

your name, and cast out demons in your name, and do many mighty works in your name?' And then will I declare to them, 'I never knew you; depart from me, you workers of lawlessness.' (Matthew 7:21 - 23)

Doing God's will is not only what God wants and is important: it is a matter of life and death. We Christians dream of that glorious moment when we will see our Savior face to face in His precious presence, and we long to meet His smile and His embrace. Our hearts are filled with hope for that moment in which Jesus will celebrate with us for having achieved it, for having persevered until that moment.

Don't you think it would be a horrible disappointment if otherwise, instead of smiling and hugging us, He claims that he doesn't know us?

What makes the difference between one situation and the other? The difference is not who has gone to church or learned the correct doctrine.

The person who enters the kingdom of heaven is the one who does the will of God.

Doing His will is not that difficult. God wants you to know and do His will.

But he who enters by the door is the shepherd of the sheep. To him the gatekeeper opens. The sheep hear his voice, and he calls his own sheep by name and leads them out. When he has brought out all his own, he goes before them, and the sheep follow him, for they know his voice. A stranger they will not follow, but they will flee from him, for they do not know the voice of strangers." (John 10:2 - 5)

Jesus is presenting Himself here as the Good Shepherd. The figure He presents is very eloquent and full of immense tenderness, which reflects the intense love He feels for his disciples.

Did you also notice that he calls *his own sheep* by name? The Good Shepherd knows you. He knows perfectly everything that has happened and is happening in your life. He knows you and calls you by name. Open your heart and listen to Him, please. I don't know what kind of emotion this produces in you, but tears come to me when I feel so loved, so important to my Lord and Savior.

Those of us who are in Jesus are under His watchful eye, and He guides us.

Also, *the sheep follow him, for they know his voice.*

This is not a minor detail when it comes to our relationship with Jesus. If you are one of His sheep, you will recognize His voice. That is, Jesus will speak to you, He will show you where to go along the path of life, and you will know how to recognize His voice among all the voices that seek to influence your life.

Do you hear the voice of Jesus? Can you recognize His voice?

Jesus' sheep do not follow strangers, nor are they carried away by the spirits of error that confuse those who stray from the truth.

Jesus himself promised not to leave us in confusion.

> *Again Jesus spoke to them, saying, "I am the light of the world. Whoever follows me will not walk in darkness, but will have the light of life."* (John 8:12)

Jesus is not one more of the crowd. He is *the light of the world*. As such, He has all the authority to declare what will happen to those who follow Him.

Those who follow Jesus are not in the dark .

If you follow Jesus, you don't have to be confused. The truth is that the disciples of Jesus live in relationship with the Invisible, but that does not mean that they live confused, without knowing what to do or what decision to make. We do not live in the dark, because we live with the light and *we have the light of life,* which is our own Savior.

Do you have Jesus in your life? Then you should know that God wants to direct your life, and that He wants to reveal to you what decision to make, so that you can live choosing to walk in obedience to Him, according to His will.

3. Pause and Seek God's Direction and Confirmation to Live in His Will.

If you walk with Jesus, you cannot walk through life letting yourself be carried away by any influence around you. You have to live according to God's will, in obedience to Him, listening to His voice and recognizing it.

Jesus' disciples pray saying:

> *… your will be done, on earth as it is in heaven.*
> (Matthew 6:10)

That is a well-known phrase from the Lord's Prayer. Many people are able to remember and repeat it, but not all really subject their lives to the will of God. We need to pray like this and then be attentive to God's voice, because He wants to direct us.

This is what happened to Gideon. If you consider this part of his story in human terms, you may consider him a little incredulous or distrustful but, would that be the case?

> *Now all the Midianites and the Amalekites and the people of the East came together, and they crossed the Jordan and encamped in the Valley of Jezreel.*

But the Spirit of the Lord clothed Gideon, and he sounded the trumpet, and the Abiezrites were called out to follow him. And he sent messengers throughout all Manasseh, and they too were called out to follow him. And he sent messengers to Asher, Zebulun, and Naphtali, and they went up to meet them.

Then Gideon said to God,

"If you will save Israel by my hand, as you have said, behold, I am laying a fleece of wool on the threshing floor. If there is dew on the fleece alone, and it is dry on all the ground, then I shall know that you will save Israel by my hand, as you have said."

And it was so. When he rose early next morning and squeezed the fleece, he wrung enough dew from the fleece to fill a bowl with water.

Then Gideon said to God,

"Let not your anger burn against me; let me speak just once more. Please let me test just once more with the fleece. Please let it be dry on the fleece only, and on all the ground let there be dew."

And God did so that night; and it was dry on the fleece only, and on all the ground there was dew. (Judges 6:33 - 40)

Gideon was not an unbeliever. He was a person like you and me, with a faith that needed confirmation as to what God wanted to do.

God had invited him to participate in His plan to answer the desperate prayer of the Israelites and deliver them from the oppression of their enemies. In response, after making sure that God was speaking to him, he made some risky decisions: he tore down the pagan altars of his people, and when enemy armies allied to invade the region he summoned as many as possible to join him in going against them.

But Gideon was a person like you and me. He was about to surrender to the conquest of an immense challenge for him, one for which he did not feel prepared or sufficient. When the Israelites began to respond to his call to fight that war, he seemed to have doubted that this was truly God's will.

What if he was wrong? It would have been a disaster for him, his family, his people and his nation! That could have ended in the extermination of Israel as a nation.

Gideon felt the need to make sure he was counting on God's backing. He wanted to confirm that he was doing His will.

What he proposed to God sounds like something he thought carefully about. It seems as if he wondered what impossible thing he could ask God to do to confirm His support.

Then he prayed to God telling Him about the wool fleece.

Gideon knew the climate of his land. He would have grown up seeing a hundred times the dew covering the floor and everything on it when he got up in the morning. He knew that what he was proposing to God was impossible. If dew fell, it would wet everything, not just the fleece.

That morning he may have gotten up anxious to see the result. If it was me, I would not have slept wondering if God would thus manifest His will. When he got up he must have run to see the fleece that he had intentionally left spread out under the night sky.

I was drenched. It wasn't just wet. He had to squeeze it to remove the water. But the ground around it was completely dry.

But then his faith stumbled once more. Just like ours, so many times. What if that was nothing more than a coincidence? What if someone had passed by that night carrying a bucket of water and tripped over wetting the fleece?

So he asked God to confirm—once again—his support by doing something even more impossible than the above. The fleece would be there again, under the night sky. What he was asking now was for the ground to be damp but the fleece to remain dry.

And so it happened.

Do you find in this passage any rebuke to Gideon for his unbelief? No, there is not. You will only find the manifestation of God's patience to deal with His son and feed his faith.

That is exactly what God wants to do with you.

God created you. There's no doubt that he knows how to deal with human beings like us, exposed to confusion, in need of a confirmation of His will that feeds our faith so that we can walk in His will.

The important thing is this: Gideon wanted to do God's will. He did not want to be carried away by the enthusiasm of his family or friends, he did not settle for the advice of those around him. He wanted to be sure that he was doing God's will and had His support.

Do you also want to do God's will?

You can do like Gideon right now. Ask God to reveal you what to do. Ask God to speak to your heart, to be the powerful influence that renews your thoughts and leads you in the sense of His will.

Today, around you, God is doing something. It may not be about to set your people militarily free from the oppression of enemies, but I assure you that God is doing something around you, and He wants you to participate in his powerful plans.

Of course, the works of God are great, according to the

greatness of His power and resources. God's works are not projects that can be accomplished with our limited human resources. That is why we need faith to live doing His will.

Let God renew your thoughts.

> *Do not be conformed to this world, but be transformed by the renewal of your mind, that by testing you may discern what is the will of God, what is good and acceptable and perfect.* (Romans 12: 2)

Jesus' sheep recognize His voice, and He promised they would not walk in the dark.

If you are not entirely sure, seek God and ask for His confirmation. He delights in those who really want to walk in His ways and carry out His plans.

Just as God confirmed to Gideon His support and His will, so He will also do with you. I have no doubt that He will.

Stop reading. Start praying, and let God lead your steps.

The Impossible As Part of Your Life

Wherever you are, you are not alone. No, apart from those who may be around you materially, there is more. Whether you feel it or not, there is a spiritual world that goes beyond our senses but is absolutely real.

And trust me: you are not alone.

Those of us who have believed in Jesus count His promises as secure. We have believed God when He told us that He was not going to leave us at any time. So that if you are one of Jesus' disciples, you should know that God's presence is with you, right now, where you are. God's gaze is upon you, knowing every detail of your life, attentive to your movements, your feelings, your thoughts, each of your steps.

And God is doing something.

Yes, God is not *idle* . The same God who promised to be with you without leaving you or forsaking you is doing something, something that affects your life and the lives of others around you.

Of course, what God does is great, really great, according to His greatness. God's works are not like human endeavors, limited by our resources and capabilities.

God is doing something great. God is deeply involved on

saving those who are being robbed, killed, and destroyed by the devil.

God's project is immense, powerful, mighty.

I think that the fact that God is doing something great and powerful is not something that surprises us very much. See what He did in six days when He created everything we see. So it's no wonder that God is doing something great.

What is surprising is that God, by doing such a great work that He is carrying out, wants to put you to work alongside Him.

Let's see, if you want, read again what I just wrote. Because this is *really* what is happening. God wants to make *you*—yes, you—part of His project; He wants to integrate you into His work team, He wants to count on you to do His work.

Yes, I thought the same as you (you, me and many others): "Who? Me? It's a joke, right? Doesn't God know me? Doesn't He know how I am?"

Sometimes it is difficult for us to understand this reality. Because, to tell the truth, is it that God cannot do His work without us?

> Can't God do His work without my offerings, my time, or my works?

> Can't God do what He wants to do without my participation?

> Can't God carry out His plan without counting on me?

I think you know the answers to these questions very well. God can do His work without you. But He has chosen to do it with you. That's what He created you for.

At the same time, God wants it to be perfectly clear that the work to be done is His, completely His, God's work and not man's, and He is doing it for our own good.

Think about that as you consider this part of Gideon's story.

Then Jerubbaal (that is, Gideon) and all the people who were with him rose early and encamped beside the spring of Harod. And the camp of Midian was north of them, by the hill of Moreh, in the valley.

The Lord said to Gideon,

"The people with you are too many for me to give the Midianites into their hand, lest Israel boast over me, saying, 'My own hand has saved me.' Now therefore proclaim in the ears of the people, saying, 'Whoever is fearful and trembling, let him return home and hurry away from Mount Gilead.' "

Then 22,000 of the people returned, and 10,000 remained. And the Lord said to Gideon,

"The people are still too many. Take them down to the water, and I will test them for you there, and anyone of whom I say to you, 'This one shall go with you,' shall go with you, and anyone of whom I say to you, 'This one shall not go with you,' shall not go."

So he brought the people down to the water. And the Lord said to Gideon,

"Every one who laps the water with his tongue, as a dog laps, you shall set by himself. Likewise, every one who kneels down to drink."

And the number of those who lapped, putting their hands to their mouths, was 300 men, but all the rest of the people knelt down to drink water.

And the Lord said to Gideon,

"With the 300 men who lapped I will save you and give the Midianites into your hand, and let all the others go every man to his home."

So the people took provisions in their hands, and their trumpets. And he sent all the rest of Israel every man to his tent, but retained the 300 men. And the camp of Midian was below him in the valley. (Judges 7: 1 - 8)

Do you know what the size of the works that God wants to do is called for us? It's called *impossible*. From our human point of view and according to what we are capable of doing, God's work is *impossible*. Impossible for us, but not impossible for God.

This is what Gideon was facing at the time. He had had an encounter with God, and in that encounter God had revealed to him that He was about to do something that up to that moment for Gideon was radically impossible. God had come down to answer the prayers of His children and was coming to deliver His people from the oppression of their enemies.

The interesting part was that He wanted Gideon to participate in this work. Again, could He do it without Gideon? Of course! But He chose to do it with him, He decided to integrate him into His team and give him a share in what He was about to do.

In the same way, God wants to work with you, in you, and through you at this time. Because also today, as well as in the time of Gideon, God is doing something great, and He wants you to participate in His work. Although His work is impossible for you.

God *can* not only do the impossible. He *chooses to* do the impossible.

For what? To make it absolutely clear that He was the one who did it. God does not want to share His glory with anyone, and He wants to be known.

If you had the opportunity to choose between conforming to the results of what you can do according to your personal abilities and resources or experiencing the manifestation and results of God's power in your life and circumstances (like in the miraculous catch, **Luke 5: 1 - 11**), what would you prefer?

Let's analyze the situation Gideon found himself in. What strikes you about this passage? (I encourage you to think about it yourself before I tell you what impacts me).

Gideon had received confirmation that God was calling him to participate in His work for the liberation of Israel from the oppression of their enemies. Then he makes a call to his neighbors and fellow citizens and they begin to arrive to participate in the resistance against the oppressors. This is how an army of thirty-two thousand soldiers gathers.

Not bad, don't you think? If I had been Gideon, I would already be considering that that response to the summons *was already God's response*. Of course! Who said there was no army? Who said there was no fighting spirit against oppression? Gideon may well have been pleasantly surprised by his summoning power.

Maybe Gideon, but not God.

Let me share with you what are the words that impact me from this passage:

The Lord said to Gideon,

> "*The people with you are too many for me to give the Midianites into their hand, lest Israel boast over me, saying, 'My own hand has saved me.'*

God saw what was happening, and had considered the number of people who had gathered for the battle, and had a different perspective than Gideon, those assembled or you and me could have.

Because, think about it, *too many people*? The above account makes it clear that the enemy's army was innumerable. Doesn't logic tell us that the more there are to face them the better?

Yes, logic, human logic. But here we are relating with God.

God was not leading Gideon in a self-esteem recovery program, suggesting encouraging phrases like "You can", "Go ahead and you will." God was leading Gideon to meet Him. He was not *informing* Gideon what He was like ("Look, Gideon, you have to know that I am great, powerful, full of authority, and that I have dominion over all things"). God wanted Gideon and everyone around him (and indeed many more, even to us today) to know Him in person, by experience.

God is not hiding. He wants to be known, He wants you to know Him, and that is why He invites you to participate in His work, so that you know who He is, how He is, not only theoretically but also in practice.

Whatever situation you are facing at this time, you have to know this: if you have placed your faith in Jesus, you have credited all the powerful promises of God, and He is faithful to His promises. God wants you to know Him and He is going to manifest Himself in the midst of the circumstances you are facing. As difficult as the situation may seem, you have to know that God wants to work beyond the impossible, in your life and through you.

About this God, the God of Gideon, the one who sent Jesus to die in our place to save us, the angel Gabriel said to Mary:

For nothing will be impossible with God. (Luke 1:37)

God Himself came to Jeremiah many years ago and said:

"Behold, I am the Lord, the God of all flesh. Is anything too hard for me? (Jeremiah 32:27)

You need to understand this: God delights in your knowing Him—in practice, by experience—as the Almighty, the One for whom nothing is impossible.

Now, have you noticed what God is emphasizing in his dealings with Gideon by minimizing his army?

*The people with you are too many **for me to give** the Midianites into their hand …*

With the 300 men who lapped **I will save you and give** the Midianites into your hand …

God was making it clear that the work they were about to see, and were going to participate in, was *HIS* work.

This reminds me of the words of Psalm 46.

"Be still, and know that I am God. I will be exalted among the nations, I will be exalted in the earth!" (Psalms 46:10)

God calls us to recognize that *He is God*, not us. We do not know how, we cannot and we do not have to try to take His place. Only He is God.

At God's initiative, Gideon's army went from thirty-two thousand soldiers to three hundred bold fellows.

The words of Andrew when Jesus was about to multiply the five loaves and two fish among a crowd of thousands ring in my mind:

... but what are they for so many? (John 6: 9).

It was the same with the scrawny army that was left in charge of Gideon. It was not enough, humanly speaking, to face the immense crowd that opposed them and that was camped not far from there.

Pay attention to this, because God works like this in your life too.

God is leading you to operate to the minimum of your resources so that you know Him, so that you see the greatness of His power and that you recognize that His work is only His. And the fact that you participate in it is a privilege that He has granted you.

Have you also noticed that there is no complaint from Gideon here when God directs him to reduce his army? Gideon is silent. He saves his words and opinions and simply obeys. Did Gideon understand what God was doing and why He was doing it that way? I don't think he fully understood it.

But let me tell you that this Gideon whom we have sometimes judged as an unbeliever for asking God to confirm His will and His support has all my respect and is a model of faith for me. I hope he is for you too.

This is the man who was hiding from his enemies, trying to rescue something to eat. He is the same one who questioned whether God was with him or with his people, given the situation in which they found themselves.

However, here you have him. When God commanded him

to send 22,000 back to their homes, he did so without question. When God proposed that he get rid of 9,700 more, he simply obeyed. And he set out to face a very large army with a handful of men.

I hope that the message that God wants to convey to you through this old story is becoming clear to you. It doesn't matter how little you have. It doesn't matter what you lack. It does not matter if what you have is insufficient to face the challenge that lies ahead. If God is with you, none of these "impossibilities" will be a limitation to what God is doing and is going to do in your life.

Think of it like this:

1. What does God want you to do?

    a. It will look difficult, maybe VERY difficult. If you want, use the word: *impossible*, if it weren't because God is doing it.

    b. You have the privilege that God has invited you to participate in His work. That work of God can be the strengthening of your marriage so that as a couple you are a testimony to many. It can be your strength in the midst of illness. It can be a financial challenge when you don't have it and can't figure out where to get what it takes. But God invited you to participate in *His work*. He is God and He will be the one who strengthens the couple, who provides the strength, who performs the miracles that are necessary so that the time comes to cover the expenses. God is the one who will bring salvation to others through you, even if it seems difficult.

    c. You have the privilege of trusting Him and His promises.

2. What do you have to achieve it?

   a. You have resources, ideas, time, concepts, plans.
   b. Now, forget about your ideas, your plans. Let God be God. Give Him everything you have and put yourself in His hands. You can depend on God.
   c. Your job is to believe in Him. Look for Him, with intensity. God is speaking to you; listen to His voice. Trust and obey. He knows what He's doing, even if you don't understand it now.

3. What is God asking you to give up (your resources, your strengths) to know his power and grace?
   The answer to that question has to be yours.

   a. God wants to do something in your life, something in which you will have to recognize that only He could do it.
   b. The knowledge of God is much more than an intellectual task. God wants you to know Him by experience.
   c. God wants to intervene, participate, show you His presence, His love and His power in the circumstances that surround you.
   d. What God is going to do will profoundly affect not only your life but the lives of many more.

Don't be scared by how little you have and the size of the challenge. God knows what He's doing.

Trust.

May the confidence that filled Gideon's heart fill yours as well.

God Wants to Increase Your Faith

What is God doing in your life at this time?

Can you perceive the hand of God operating in your life?

This is something that we can sometimes overlook. Today, God wants to call your attention to make you notice that He is working in your life and around you. Think about it seriously, meditate on the things that have been happening, your relationships, what you have felt, the things that have impacted you in some way. God is working. God is present in what is happening to you.

God knows our heart, to the core. He wants us to live in His will. And that is precisely what is best for us! How often do we err in thinking that we benefit by following the course of our own plans, in which we do not consider God! That is a terrible deception!

However, God is patient, and there He is, next to you, giving you a new opportunity to decide by His will instead of yours.

There is something that must also be clear to us: living in God's will implies living by faith.

Faith is the missing ingredient in our life. For some reason it seems good to us to live according to our own reasoning (influenced by others, by the media, by the world in general). But today God wants to call us back to live with Him, according to His will, supported by faith in Him.

Yes, it is a great challenge.

Why? Because the works that God does—the ones He did, the ones He is doing, and the ones He will do—are great. They do not represent a challenge for Him, but for us they are impossible. However, He directs us to participate in His works so that we know Him, so that we experience what is beyond our capacities and resources, because He created us to live in a close relationship with Him.

Wasn't this what happened to the great figures in the Bible?

- God revealed himself to Moses when he was about to answer the prayers of His people to free them from slavery in Egypt. The work to be done was immense, absolutely impossible for anyone. But God used Moses, a mere mortal like you and me, who could experience over and over again the mighty hand of God moving in his life and around him.

- God manifested Himself to the prophet Elijah when He wanted to show the people of Israel that He was the true God. The people were being confused and seduced by paganism, and many were doubting between God and the pagan deities of the surrounding towns. What did God use in Elijah's life to convince the people? Did He provide nice words and convincing arguments to win a discussion? No. God brought fire down from heaven to prove that He is the true God, and He did so in response to a simple prayer from Elijah. Can you imagine God bringing fire down from heaven in response to one of **your** prayers? That is what He did, and both Elijah and many recognized the true God.

- When God wanted to fulfill His promise to deliver the Promised Land to the people of Israel, he also associated Himself with a man, Joshua. Israel's was not the most powerful army on the planet, on the contrary, it was very far from that. Joshua and the people saw God's miracles over and over as they lived out the fulfillment of His promises, thus knowing the true, powerful God who loves His people. The challenge was of divine proportions, and God used this humble human being to overcome it.

- When God wanted to reveal the way of salvation to many, He manifested Himself clearly and commissioned a handful of men and women without much preparation and without resources. Homework? To be witnesses of the resurrection of His Son and to carry the message of salvation as far as possible. The result? Many centuries later you are one of the millions of people who are receiving something from Jesus and being touched by the presence, grace and power of the One who has wanted to save us. From any point of view that was an impossible mission for that humble group of people, but they, and all those who came after, experienced the power and grace of God working in their lives and around them.

And now it's your turn. Now is the time for you to experience what God is doing, because He continues to work to this day.

God wants you to know Him, to walk with Him, to see Him working in your life. That is why I remind you of the question from the beginning:

What is God doing in your life at this time?

Pay attention, because God is working, in you and around you.

It's obvious that to undertake the work of God, to associate with Him and participate in what He's doing, it requires faith.

Sometimes we think that "that kind of faith" is reserved for a few, for a few elite of called and elevated who achieve a closeness with God out of the ordinary. What God wants you to understand is that "that kind of faith" is what He wants you to have.

God wants to feed your faith.

God wants to give you everything you need to believe, to trust in His presence and His power, so that you can take on the challenges of faith that He is putting before you.

Any of us can say that we are nobody, that we are persons full of limitations and weaknesses. So did Moses, and Gideon repeated it.

But God insists, and wants to encourage us to participate in His work.

Consider what happened to Gideon and his small army (could it be called that?) after God reduced their number to no more than three hundred.

That same night the Lord said to him,

"Arise, go down against the camp, for I have given it into your hand. But if you are afraid to go down, go down to the camp with Purah your servant. And you shall hear what they say, and afterward your hands shall be strengthened to go down against the camp."

Then he went down with Purah his servant to the outposts of the armed men who were in the camp. And the Midianites and the Amalekites and all the people of the East lay along the valley like locusts in abundance, and their camels were without number, as the sand that is on the seashore in abundance. When

*Gideon came, behold, a man was telling a dream to
his comrade.*

And he said,

*"Behold, I dreamed a dream, and behold, a cake of
barley bread tumbled into the camp of Midian and
came to the tent and struck it so that it fell and turned
it upside down, so that the tent lay flat."*

And his comrade answered,

*"This is no other than the sword of Gideon the son of
Joash, a man of Israel; God has given into his hand
Midian and all the camp."*

*As soon as Gideon heard the telling of the dream and
its interpretation, he worshiped. And he returned to
the camp of Israel and said,*

*"Arise, for the Lord has given the host of Midian into
your hand."* (Judges 7: 9-15)

The first thing I would like you to notice in this story is that
God makes it clear that *He* is the one doing something. He is not
asking Gideon to do the work He cannot do. God is about to act
and only asks Gideon to be there, to accompany Him:

*… for **I have given** it into your hand.*

Who is going to do it? Who is going to free the people of Israel
from their oppressors? Is God asking Gideon to do it? No! God
makes it clear at all times that it is He who is doing the work.

In the same way God wants to work in your life. What God

is doing in you and around you is immense, impossible to do with your resources or possibilities. It is something that only God can do and could perfectly do without your intervention. But God wanted to work in you and through you. He is giving you the opportunity to know His power, His grace, His love, His authority.

God is doing something in your family, something that is beyond what you could do. God is working in the lives and families of the people you work with. God is working in your community. He wants to save, forgive, restore, show His love and grace. It is too big a work for you. What God is doing is at His level. But God is relating with you and wants to use you to do His work.

Are you going to argue that you are weak, inadequate or that you do not have the necessary resources? Do you think that God does not know?

Do you think that God did not know that Gideon did not have what it took to defeat that immense army that was coming against them?

God knows how small we are. He knows about our poverty, our weakness and our ignorance. But He has chosen to work in us and through us.

So **God wants you to live by faith** . He wants you to trust Him even when you don't understand what He's doing. You have to trust that He knows what He's doing, and He Himself wants to feed your faith, giving you the ability to trust Him in that way.

That is what He did in Gideon's life. In Judges chapter eight we learn that the army of the Midianites was of one hundred and thirty-five thousand soldiers. Against *three hundred*? Yes, that sounds ridiculous. Of course it is impossible in human terms, but not for God.

Challenges may arise in your life that sound just as ridiculous as the one Gideon faced. The same God who touched Gideon's life and called him to participate in the deliverance of His people is working in your life right now. What God is doing today is also as great as what He was doing in Gideon's time.

What does it take from you?

Gideon needed faith and courage to face such a situation. You need the same.

But how does someone get to have such kind of faith?

God wants to feed your faith, just as He fed Gideon's faith.

Because, how did Gideon have that faith, that confidence that allowed him to go with three hundred to a battle against one hundred and thirty-five thousand?

God gave it to him. Faith never stops being a gift from God.

See how God nurtured Gideon's faith. God knew his heart, just as He knows yours.

… if you are afraid to go down …

God knew exactly what Gideon was feeling. If I had been in his place I would also have been in shock. That could have been the end for Gideon and his men.

That is why God wanted to encourage Gideon, He wanted to fill his heart with the confidence necessary to face the challenge. God wants to do the same with you.

How did God strengthen Gideon's faith?

He sent him to spy on the camp of the Midianites. He sent him to listen to what the enemies were saying.

Consider carefully what happened to Gideon at that time, because God is going to work in similar ways in your life.

Gideon, accepting God's offer to help him overcome his fear, went to the camp of his enemies just as God told him. The army of the Midianites and their allies consisted of one hundred and thirty-five thousand armed men, so imagine how Gideon and Fura must have felt when they compared that camp with their own, which they had just left behind.

There is a phrase in the story that I find very revealing.

> *When Gideon came, behold, a man was telling a dream to his comrade.*

Do you know what we call this type of situation? We call it *coincidence*, or maybe *chance*.

In other words, Gideon arrived *just* at that moment.

He could have arrived when ...

- ... The enemy soldiers made war exercises with their weapons.
- ... The same tent neighbors talked, showing off all the enemies they had defeated or what they had done to them.
- ... The guards laughed out loud mocking the weakness of Gideon and his army.

They could have arrived at any other time. But no, they arrived *precisely, coincidentally* (what a *coincidence!*), at the moment when the men interpreted the dream of one of them, anticipating that their own army would be defeated by the small handful of men led by Gideon.

Was it a coincidence? Was that just a coincidence?

I guess you answered no. Gideon also did not interpret it as a mere coincidence.

> *As soon as Gideon heard the telling of the dream and its interpretation, he worshiped.*

Have you ever been through a time or situation in which you had to acknowledge without a doubt that God was at work? That is what happened to Gideon. He arrived *"by chance"* at the moment when they said something that concerned him and a lot, and he could not help but recognize that God was there, that God was speaking to him, that He was confirming His intervention in that situation, that He was feeding his faith and giving him the courage to face whatever came, although he was still not quite clear on what it would be.

When you walk in God's will, when you live in an authentic, everyday relationship with Him, things like this happen to you. Some might call them chance, coincidences, "things of destiny." Those of us who believe in Jesus recognize the loving and powerful intervention of our heavenly Father to touch our hearts, edify our souls, and increase our faith.

Please, stop treating things that happen to you as coincidences. Begin to see God and what He is doing right where you are, where He put you, in the relationships He has given you and in the events that occur in your life and around you.

You could reinforce this concept using the life story of any other of the biblical characters. This intervention of God in the lives of people is something recurrent, which not only happened in the life of Gideon, but has occurred and occurs in the lives of millions of people until today.

Many years ago there was a couple who were engaged to be married. But a series of events occurred that transformed their plans into something completely different from what they had imagined. His name was Joseph, she was called Mary.

Their lives seemed to be developing normally, and they had their plans, each one in particular and also plans in common. But then God stepped in and changed everything. So they had to stop living "in their own way", according to their plan, and a completely different panorama opened up for them, absolutely challenging, with implications that infinitely exceeded what they were capable of conceiving.

Mary was visited by an angel who announced that she would be the mother of the Savior, and that this would happen without human intervention. She submitted to divine design and found herself pregnant overnight without having had intercourse with her fiancé. Everything had changed for her.

One day Joseph found out that his fiancée was expecting a baby, and you can imagine the first conclusions he may have reached. He may have felt betrayed, cheated, taken for a fool. But God was doing something in the midst of all that situation, and He wanted to make Joseph part of His work as well. An angel appeared to him in a dream and invited him to believe, encouraged him to go ahead with his wedding plans even though he did not clearly understand what was happening. Joseph believed. Joseph and Mary got married and went through the process together towards the birth of that miraculous baby.

Was something of what happened to them a coincidence?

Was it nothing more than chance that the Roman emperor, a political leader who lived thousands of miles away from where they were, ordered a census to be taken just as she was facing the final period of her pregnancy? Was it by chance that they came to the town of Bethlehem when there was no accommodation available? Was it a coincidence that humble shepherds were grazing their sheep on the night of the birth and were visited by angels?

No! A hundred thousand times no! None of this was by chance. It was the hand of God, present and powerful, outlining the design of **His plan.**

The same plan that God is carrying out to this day, right where you are.

Are you not feeling invited to consider the conversations

around you much more carefully? What if God wanted to use one of them to feed your faith just as He fed Gideon's?

God keeps working and keeps calling. God continues to build people of faith.

You cannot be a Christian and not live by faith.

... for we walk by faith, not by sight. (2 Corinthians 5:7)

And without faith it is impossible to please him, for whoever would draw near to God must believe that he exists and that he rewards those who seek him. (Hebrews 11: 6)

For in it the righteousness of God is revealed from faith for faith, as it is written, "The righteous shall live by faith." (Romans 1:17)

As I already told you, now it is your turn.

Do you live by faith?

To what extent do you believe God?

I didn't ask you *to what extent do you believe in God*, but *to what extent **do you believe God***. God promised to be with you, God forgave your sins when you believed in Jesus.

God wants to get even more into your life. He wants to intervene by doing what you have not even been able to imagine.

Trust God, lean on His promises and live obeying Him, even if you don't always understand what He is doing or why He is doing it. Trust. He does know the why and He is doing a perfect work for which He has decided to count on you.

Trust, and you will know God as you have never known Him before.

The Victory, According to God

What needs to happen for you to experience such an impressive victory that a new revelation from God profoundly impacts your life?

If we talk about victory, we are talking about conflict. There is no victory without opposition. So what obstacles do you face? What difficulties do you have ahead? Or, perhaps going a little deeper: What powerful work does God want to do in the context of your family and your community using you?

I know these are difficult questions to answer. However, it is important that you analyze and meditate on them yourself. I invite you to reflect on this because I am convinced that God is doing something in your life, and around you. Children of God are not on vacation during our lives in the flesh. From the moment we are reconciled to God by believing in Jesus, we become involved in God's work, adjusting ourselves to live in His will.

Today we don't talk much about victories, we talk about success. What describes successful people? What would success look like in your life? The world defines success in terms of numbers: how much money is in bank accounts, position in the company ladder, number of followers on social media, and so on. That changes radically when a person believes in Jesus. Once Jesus is your Savior and the Owner of your life, and when you establish a relationship with God, success is defined differently. We are disciples of the

One who did not come to be served but to serve, the one who taught that the greatest in the Kingdom of Heaven are those who serve others. That is why those of us who follow Jesus have to redefine victory according to these terms.

The disciple of Jesus experiences victory when the power of God is more evident than his own actions. He gets involved, works, participates, but what makes it possible for what he works for to come to completion is God's intervention. The child of God comes to experience and know his heavenly Father by seeing how the impossible becomes reality through the work of the Mighty One.

Do you want to experience victory that way? Does the idea of knowing God more and better through His miraculous and powerful intervention in your life inspire you?

That is the exact position where God is leading you, because He delights in your knowing Him and rejoicing in Him. That was what happened to Gideon when he confidently surrendered himself to God's will and saw the impossible materialize before his own eyes. It's what I think God has prepared for you too.

And he [Gideon] *divided the 300 men into three companies and put trumpets into the hands of all of them and empty jars, with torches inside the jars.*

And he said to them,

"Look at me, and do likewise. When I come to the outskirts of the camp, do as I do. When I blow the trumpet, I and all who are with me, then blow the trumpets also on every side of all the camp and shout, 'For the Lord and for Gideon.' "

So Gideon and the hundred men who were with him came to the outskirts of the camp at the beginning of

*the middle watch, when they had just set the watch.
And they blew the trumpets and smashed the jars that
were in their hands. Then the three companies blew
the trumpets and broke the jars. They held in their
left hands the torches, and in their right hands the
trumpets to blow. And they cried out, "A sword for the
Lord and for Gideon!" Every man stood in his place
around the camp, and all the army ran. They cried out
and fled. When they blew the 300 trumpets, the Lord
set every man's sword against his comrade and against
all the army. And the army fled as far as Beth-shittah
toward Zererah, as far as the border of Abel-meholah,
by Tabbath.* (Judges 7.16–22)

1.   A Risky and Decisive Leadership.

Let me introduce you to the new Gideon. Yes, this Gideon almost seems to be another person, different from the one we met at the beginning of the story.

It has probably happened to you that you have met a person you had not seen for a long time, and you almost have to ask him or her: "Is it really you?" There are changes for the better, and changes for the worse, but the truth is that we are all changing. The situations and problems we face, circumstances, relationships, and much more, all are factors that promote our transformation. But it's a really wonderful thing when it's God who transforms us.

When you meet God face to face in Jesus Christ, when you truly experience the impact of His presence and receive the revelation of His greatness, love, grace and power, you cannot help but be transformed.

"And we all, with unveiled face, beholding the glory of the Lord, are being transformed into the same image from one degree of glory to another. For this comes from the Lord who is the Spirit". (2 Corinthians 3:18)

At the beginning of the account, in Judges 6:15, Gideon resists the Lord's call by describing himself:

And he said to him, "Please, Lord, how can I save Israel? Behold, my clan is the weakest in Manasseh, and I am the least in my father's house."

How would you describe this person? We can say that he was insecure, that he did not feel capable of facing the challenge that was presented to him, that he did not believe that he could do it. Listen to yourself in his words, because that is how you have felt too. You have not felt up to what God wants to do, and you have excused yourself by suggesting that you do not have the necessary preparation, that you do not occupy an important position or that you do not have the resources that would be needed.

The interesting thing is that the story did not end there, with Gideon's timid description of himself, because he was willing to consider what God was telling him.

That same Gideon, the most insignificant of the weakest clan of the tribe of Manasseh:

- Had openly opposed the idolatry of his own family and community by breaking down and setting fire to the idols that his own father had established.
- Had summoned war against the enemies, gathering around him an army of thirty-two thousand soldiers.
- Had had the audacity—let me please give it that name—to reduce his army by sending home more than 99% of his

soldiers, leaving only three hundred men to face an enemy army of one hundred and thirty-two thousand.

As if all that was not enough, analyze his behavior in this story:

And he [Gideon] *divided the 300 men into three companies and put trumpets into the hands of all of them and empty jars, with torches inside the jars.*

And he said to them,

"Look at me, and do likewise. When I come to the outskirts of the camp, do as I do. When I blow the trumpet, I and all who are with me, then blow the trumpets also on every side of all the camp and shout, 'For the Lord and for Gideon.'"

There you have him, officiating as a general, giving instructions to his people. What you see here is a determined man, risky, launching himself into battle like a person who has nothing to lose. "Look at me; follow my example," he tells them. He does not send them into danger while he remains at home, but instead sets out to go ahead of them, establishing the pattern they should follow.

Do you understand what you read? You are considering the performance of a transformed person. But what was it that transformed Gideon? Ask yourself, please, because it could be what can transform your own life too.

Gideon was transformed by God. I think we all agree on that. The shy man who hid the harvest while lamenting his bad luck and that of his family is now a fearless general who acts as if a thousand battles have taught him what to do.

A. **Gideon Had an Encounter With God.** There are experiences that transform people. Psychologists call them "traumatic experiences", and they are those that leave a permanent result in the lives of those who live them. Everything seemed "normal" in Gideon's life, until God crossed his path, changing everything. Suddenly, in God's own presence, he understood that his perspective on reality could be wrong, and he received a call from God. The Creator wanted to use him to do something awesome, which was going to affect the lives of everyone around him (including us). It was hard for him to believe, his transformation was not immediate, but the seeds of the Word that God sowed in his heart had produced a safe and abundant harvest. Doesn't that sound like the parable of the grounds that Jesus taught? This is the way God continues to work in those who have an encounter with Him.

B. **Gideon's Faith Had Developed.** When the Angel of the Lord visited him, Gideon believed in God, but he also believed that God had abandoned him, his family, and his people, and that the miracles that their elders had told them about were no longer repeated. But, do you remember what happened? He lived through a process by which God fed his faith, first confirming—at his request—that it was He who was speaking to him, and clearly responding to his insistent requests for confirmation. Finally it had been God himself who had taken the initiative to lead him to the camp of his enemies to reaffirm his conviction in what he was going to do. The difference was very clear: before, Gideon believed but did not trust, and now it can be said that he didn't simply believed, but that the assurance of what God was about to do filled his heart. When he arrived on the battlefield, Gideon was filled with an infectious confidence, capable of not doubting that God had brought them there and was going to give them victory. Do you understand how this also applies to your life? I believe that we can all go through those moments of spiritual warfare in which we can wonder if God is really there to defend us. Does God reject us for that? No, just as He did with Gideon, He reveals himself to us, encourages us, teaches us. And He does not reject us when we doubt, when we need a confirmation because we are not sure (or three confirmations), or when we do not understand. The same God who worked in Gideon's life is the one who is working in your life.

2. A Reliable Team.

When we refer to this account we always mention Gideon. It is logical that we do so, because he is the judge that God sent to His people at that time, and he is the only one who is mentioned by name. But have you ever considered the three hundred brave men who entered the camp of the hundred and thirty-two thousand armed enemies with him? They are heroes too!

I believe that all the Israelites knew the dimensions of the size of the enemy army. This is how he is described at the beginning of the story: *"For they would come up with their livestock and their tents; they would come like locusts in number—both they and their camels could not be counted—so that they laid waste the land as they came in"* (Judges 6.5). This description defines them as an irrepressible crowd.

Now imagine for a moment that you are one of the thousands of Israelites who responded to Gideon's initial call to confront the Midianites. Surely a ray of hope could have been kindled in your heart by observing that many had responded, just like you. So Gideon orders all those who are afraid to return to their homes, and you grit your teeth and propose to stay, despite the reduction of that improvised army. So Gideon takes them to the stream to drink, and after some time he starts saying something like "You can go home; but you, stay". Selection process, and you are among the chosen ones. When you look at the final group, they look like little more than a gathering of friends.

Don't you think you would have wondered how that handful of farmers was going to stand up to the countless they had against them?

Do you understand what I'm referring to? Those men had to be carriers of a faith comparable to Gideon's! If we coldly apply logic, we have to recognize that those three hundred were being invited to launch a suicide attack. We are not told that they rebelled, that they protested, or that they questioned the strategy that their leader proposed to them. They just trusted.

Actually, we can say that it was God who chose them, and of course, God knows exactly what is in people's hearts, so God knew who He was choosing.

> *"Now faith is the assurance of things hoped for, the conviction of things not seen".* (Hebrews 11:1)

Faith—that which both Gideon and these men had—is essential, to the point that without it it is impossible to please God (Hebrews 11:6). That is, if you are going to cultivate a relationship with God, you need to have faith, like them. Faith will lead you to do crazy things, blessed crazy things! These follies and their results will allow God, the invisible God, to be seen, revealed so that others can also believe in Him.

3. A Ridiculous Strategy.

Have you ever stopped to analyze Gideon's battle strategy? I guess I am not alone in giving this title ("A Ridiculous Strategy") to this section. With all due respect to General Gideon, but his strategy was ridiculous!

To begin with, the numerical difference between the two opposing groups was ridiculous. You can ask anyone: if an army of one hundred and thirty-two thousand goes against one of three hundred, which group will have the victory? In addition, the Midianites were experienced soldiers who had been fighting and crushing opponents in the area for some time. For their part, the Israelites were simple farmers, without much experience in combat, starting with their leader.

And the weapons? Well, some pots, some torches, some trumpets … Don't you consider this is a ridiculous strategy? The enemies skillfully wielded swords, spears, javelins, bows.

What I seem to understand here is that unless something very special happens, Gideon's idea was a recipe for disaster. And that is precisely where faith lies, and where it rests. This victory rests on the reality that it was not humanly possible. It depended entirely on that "something special" which is really God's intervention.

When was the last time you did something without a safety net?

You and I can feel this way at times, helpless in the face of danger, powerless in the face of challenge. But God brought us to reflect on the experience of Gideon and the people of Israel to feed our faith, because it may lead us to experience the impossible as they did.

If you stop to think about it, you will find that this is not the only story of ridiculous strategies. There is a biblical pattern that shows us God's intervention when humans cannot succeed. What would you say about the conquest of Jericho? Trumpets and shouts before a walled city? And David before Goliath? The Exodus? The feeding of the five thousand?

This is the moment when you receive the challenge. You are being called to join the army of God, the community of those who expose themselves to what is before them, trusting wholeheartedly in God, who guides and inspires them. And they are the ones who get to have the experience of seeing God in action through their hands, their feet, their voices or whatever was in their pockets! Do you want to be one of them?

4. A Miraculous Victory.

Finally, after so much pondering and analyzing this story, we reached the climax. The three hundred bravely enter, on tiptoe, the enemy camp, densely populated with heavily armed and well-trained enemies for combat. The decisive moment has arrived, and there is no other alternative. They were divided into three divisions, and Gideon makes a sign to those who go with him, about a hundred. They would have moved a little apart from each other, to make a greater impression. He had told the others to do exactly what they saw him and those with him do. They carried the trumpets in one hand and in the other the pitchers with the torches inside. Then he did it: he smashed the pitcher to the ground, raised the torch that began to flare up and glow in the darkness of the night, raised the trumpet to his mouth and blew hard. Those around him began to imitate him, so they began to hear more and more pitchers breaking and trumpets blowing, while the torches lit up. So did the other squads. Gideon must have been the first to cry out, "For the Lord and for Gideon!" And the others did the same.

That was their part.

The rest was done by God.

That is where God is taking you and me, over and over again. Our task is not to produce the miracle or bring about the victory. That is beyond our human reach. Our job is to believe and obey without question, and then trust and wait. The author of the miracle is always He, God, our Father, the one who invited us to live with Him the adventure of Christian life. May God help us so that we never forget Him, so that we never happen to take credit for the work that only He can do.

We have been invited to be in the right place, at the right time. Then we will see the glory of God.

How had Gideon felt, and how had the three hundred felt at that time? While an overdose of adrenaline tensed their muscles to the maximum, still without moving, they began to see armed men begin to emerge from the tents, surprisingly attacking whoever happened to be in front of them. Yes, as they stood there, struggling to stay in their posts and blowing trumpets from time to time, they saw them hurt and kill each other, while some, perhaps already injured, fled as if an army of a million would have caught up with them. I imagine those three hundred trembling, holding their breath, as those shocking scenes unfolded before their own astonished eyes. It was more than evident: this was God, fighting on their behalf.

This testimony is written there because they came out of that bloodbath whole and without injuries, and they could speak about it. Yes, they said they saw God, they saw the hand of God intervening in the affairs of His children, coming to their defense and responding powerfully to their cry. They saw the result of prayer and the product of obedience. And today God himself brings them to our consideration so that we can learn from their example.

What do you learn from all this?

Please, stop visiting this story just as a story. God inspired the writing of these passages so that we could see ourselves reflected in them, so that now we are the ones who occupy our rightful place, so that we, too, come to see God as they experienced Him.

I invite you to consider your own life, your history before and after believing in Jesus, what you have been living in the last time and the challenges that God has placed before you. Perhaps yourself, and probably other people as well, have prayed to God, and He is about to respond. Listen to the voice of God, who may be inviting you to be part of His answer, and trust, even if you do not understand everything. God is at work.

Do you think you have little faith? Remember that God wants to feed your faith, He wants to strengthen it. And when your confidence has reached the acceptable level, God will lead you to victory, where you can see Him, working by grace before your very eyes.

So take your breath. May God lead you to such a great victory that a new revelation of His person, His power and His grace will fill your life and your heart.

Trust. God knows what He's doing.

Printed in the United States
By Bookmasters